Arran

40 Favourite Walks

The author and publisher have made every effort to ensure that the information in this publication is accurate, and accept no responsibility whatsoever for any loss, injury or inconvenience experienced by any person or persons whilst using this book.

published by
pocket mountains ltd
Holm Street, Moffat, DG10 9EB
pocketmountains.com

ISBN: 978-1-907025-32-7

Text and photography copyright © Phil Turner

The right of Phil Turner to be identified as the Author of this work has been asserted by him in accordance with the Copyright, Designs and Patents Act 1988

A catalogue record for this book is available from the British Library

Contains Ordnance Survey data © Crown copyright and database right 2012, supported by out of copyright mapping from 1945-1961

Printed in Poland

Introduction

The Isle of Arran is often referred to as 'Scotland in Miniature', thanks to the Highland Boundary Fault which divides the island into Highland and Lowland landscapes with towering granite peaks in the north and rolling farmland in the south. This geological variety has made Arran a Mecca for geologists who visit the island to study intrusive igneous landforms such as sills and dykes as well as sedimentary and metasedimentary rocks. Palm trees overlooking peaceful sandy bays and coastal caves behind raised beaches offer plenty to tempt those seeking a contrast to the rugged drama of the Northern Hills.

This guide offers 40 moderate walks exploring every area of this compact island, from the classic ascent of Arran's highest summit Goatfell to more sedate strolls through shady forests and wild heather moorland. Despite being the largest island in the Firth of Clyde (at 432 square kilometres), the island is compact and easy to explore and many of these routes can be combined to create longer walks making use of public transport.

The routes in this book are divided into five sections, each of which is introduced by a summary giving an overview of the area and a map showing start points.

Safety
Although termed moderate walks, many are on unmarked paths and faint tracks that are rough underfoot. Appropriate footwear should be selected – the route description can help you decide. The sketch maps are just that – planning aids that should be supplemented with more detailed mapping such as that by the Ordnance Survey. Conveniently, the whole island fits onto a single map – either the OS Landranger sheet 69 at 1:50,000 scale, or OS Explorer sheet 361 at 1:25,000.

The weather on the west coast of Scotland is notoriously unpredictable and even a short walk can quickly become a major epic when the conditions change – with that in mind it is important to pack wind- and waterproof clothing and adequate warm layers to allow the walk to be completed no matter what the weather.

Many of the walks are suitable for accompanied children – some are even pushchair accessible – but a few of the walks listed are more suited to experienced walkers: judgement should be exercised.

Access
All walks are easy to reach using Arran's excellent and well integrated public transport network – though the narrow, rough roads have taken their toll on the local buses! Arran is connected with the mainland by two ferries, one from Brodick to Ardrossan and the second from Lochranza to Claonaig in summer and to Tarbert in winter. A timetabled shuttle service connects Lamlash to neighbouring Holy Isle in summer, with less frequent

crossings for the rest of the year.

The bus service is scheduled around the arrival and departure of the main ferry crossings, and buses will generally wait for a delayed ferry. This has little real impact on the laid-back nature of island life, particularly when you realise that Arran only has three roads. The 90km-long coast road – declassified for a third of its length – circumnavigates the island, only venturing inland to climb the 200m-high pass located between Sannox and Lochranza. The other two roads run across the island from east to west; the main one from Brodick to Blackwaterfoot is called The String and the minor road running from Lamlash to Lagg and Sliddery is known as The Ross. The bus runs around the coast road and The String, picking up and dropping off on demand – every walk in this book can be accessed using the bus and there really is no need to bring a car onto the island.

The Land Reform (Scotland) Act 2003 gave walkers rights of access over most of Scotland away from residential buildings, but these rights must be exercised responsibly and the Scottish Outdoor Access Code should always be followed in order to maintain cordial relationships with landowners. Keep dogs under strict control at all times and take care not to disturb birds nesting above the high-tideline on the beaches in breeding season (April-May). If walking in the autumn months, it is particularly important to make use of the Hillphones service to avoid disrupting the annual red deer stalking that takes place in the north of the island (snh.org.uk/hillphones).

Wildlife

Arran is a haven for wildlife – especially birds – with more than 200 species recorded on the island, including eider, peregrine falcon and golden eagle which are often seen soaring from the hills above Arran Distillery in Lochranza. Red squirrel can be seen darting through the canopy on woodland walks, and coastal visitors include otter, seal, harbour porpoise and even basking shark. Walkers in the Northern Hills will soon become familiar with the red deer herds, and the observant will often be rewarded with sightings of adder and common lizard.

If rarity is measured by numbers alone, Arran is home to some of the most endangered tree species in the world in the form of three species of Arran whitebeam protected within an enclosure in Gleann Diomhan. Less than 300 cut-leaved and Scottish whitebeam were recorded as mature trees in 1980, and the Catacol whitebeam was represented by just two specimens when discovered in 1997. Now monitored by Scottish Natural Heritage, a third whitebeam is rumoured to have been eaten by deer, hence the high fences!

History

Arran has been inhabited since the early Neolithic period, a race of farmers leaving evidence of their passing in the form of faint field systems and somewhat more obvious stone circles, standing stones and cairns. Whilst their exact purpose is unknown, it is safe to assume that these stone circles had some kind of ceremonial function, and the best examples are the six stone circles located on Machrie Moor. There is a particular concentration of Clyde cairns (a form of gallery grave), consisting of a rectangular or trapezoidal stone and earth mound encasing a chamber lined with larger stone slabs. Remains found inside the chambers suggest that these structures were used for rituals as well as simply for internments. There are good examples known as the Giants' Graves overlooking Whiting Bay.

Gaelic-speakers from Ireland colonised the island in the 6th century and turned it into a centre of religious activity. During the Viking Age in the 11th century, Arran was part of the Sodor (South Isles) of the Kingdom of Mann and the Isles, under the direct rule of Magnus III of Norway. Much later, in 1237, the Scottish isle broke away from the Isle of Man and became an independent kingdom before being ceded to the Scottish Crown a few decades later as a result of the Treaty of Perth. Evidence of Arran's Viking past can be seen in the form of a huge grave south of Lamlash at Kingscross, where finds included whalebone, iron and bronze hardware and a 9th-century bronze coin.

Brodick Castle dates from the 13th century, originally a seat of the Clan Stewart before passing to the Boyd family in the 15th century. A tumultuous past saw it captured by English forces during the Wars of Independence before it was taken back by Scottish troops in 1307. It was damaged by English ships in 1406 and then by John of Islay, the 'Lord of the Isles', in 1455. At the end of the 15th century James III granted Brodick Castle to James Hamilton, 1st Lord Hamilton, and his son, confusingly also called James, was made Earl of Arran by James IV in 1503. The Hamilton family remained in residence for several centuries, overseeing a gradual population growth before Alexander, 10th Duke of Hamilton, embarked on a devastating programme of Clearances in the 19th century. Alternative land and accommodation was promised in Canada for each adult emigrant male, with half their fare being paid for by the Duke. Whole villages were displaced and the Gaelic culture of the island devastated. A memorial to the displaced families has been constructed on the shore at Lamlash, paid for by a Canadian descendant of the emigrants.

Accommodation

Arran is only a small island and in the summer months accommodation can be in short supply. It's essential to book in advance and keep an eye on the busy event schedule which can wipe out the entire accommodation stock in one swoop.

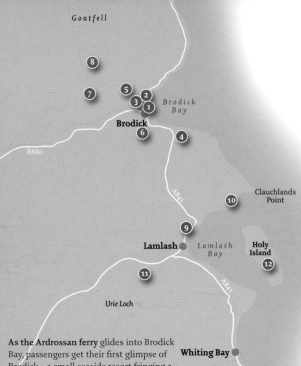

Goatfell

⑧

⑦ ⑤ ② *Brodick*
③ ① *Bay*

Brodick
⑥ ④

B880

A841

⑩ Clauchlands
Point

⑨

Lamlash *Lamlash* **Holy**
Bay **Island**
⑫

⑪

Urie Loch

A841

Whiting Bay

As the Ardrossan ferry glides into Brodick Bay, passengers get their first glimpse of Brodick – a small seaside resort fringing a wide blue bay with flashes of golden sand beneath the towering peak of Goatfell, the highest summit on Arran. Peeking out from wooded slopes, Brodick Castle is easily missed, but this strategically-important castle with its beautiful manicured gardens is a highlight of any visitor itinerary and makes the objective for several fine walks.

Heading south around Clauchlands Point, Lamlash Bay is sheltered by rugged Holy Isle, an intriguing island with a long history as a sacred site. Previous residents include the 6th-century hermit Saint Molaise and, more recently, wild Eriskay ponies and members of a Tibetan Buddhist Community.

Mountain walks in this area include the popular route from Brodick to the summit of Goatfell and the high-level ridge walk containing the Three Beinns, accessed from beautiful Glen Rosa. Low-level walks include visits to sites of historical interest such as the standing stones near Cladach and the iron age fort of Dun Fionn.

Brodick, Lamlash and Glen Rosa

TO THE FERRY ↑

The Fisherman's Walk

Distance 2km **Time** 1 hour (one way)
Terrain aggregate footpaths, grassy
tracks and a section of sandy beach
Map OS Explorer 361 or Landranger 69
Access Stagecoach buses to Brodick

**A linear walk alongside the beach and
saltmarsh from Brodick to Brodick Castle
and Country Park.**

Leave Brodick seafront by taking the
road between the white building and the
putting green, passing the children's
playground on the left with the beach to
the right. Goatfell soon comes into view,
with Brodick Castle also emerging from
the woodland ahead. At the road end, take
the track adjacent to the playing field
which narrows to a gravel path before

passing over the Glencloy Water via a
footbridge to the left. Follow the path as it
skirts an area of saltmarsh before crossing
a corner of the golf course.

Take the golf club footbridge over the
Glenrosa Water, and obey the large
warning sign by turning sharp right to
follow the river downstream. The gorse-
lined path takes you alongside the golf
course for a short distance before
emerging at Brodick's north beach.
Continue north along the golf course
(being aware of wayward golf balls) or the
sandy beach to reach the third footbridge
across the Cnocan Burn.

Turn around to steal a last look at
Brodick Bay laid out behind you, then
cross the wooden bridge into a patch of

woodland to reach the car park alongside the A841. Crossing the road gives access to the Cladach Visitor Centre and the Arran Brewery and shop, as well as the start of the Glen Rosa, Goatfell and Brodick Country Park walks.

Before the development of modern Brodick on the south side of the bay, Cladach was the main settlement in these parts and employees of the sawmill

here lived in houses, now demolished, built along the coast road. Look out for the hydro-electric scheme which takes water from a reservoir high up on the slopes of Goatfell to generate power in turbines behind the sawmill.

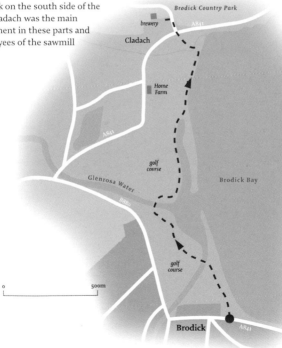

◀ Brodick Country Park across Brodick Bay

Brodick Country Park

Distance 2.6km **Time** 1 hour 30
Terrain aggregate footpaths and beaten
earth tracks; potentially muddy in places
Map OS Explorer 361 or Landranger 69
Access Stagecoach bus (324) to Cladach.
The National Trust for Scotland own
Brodick Castle and gardens and unless
you're a member you'll need to pay to visit
the castle and/or gardens

This is one of many walks through the
interconnecting trails in the woodland
surrounding Brodick Castle. Whilst this
walk offers a good taste of the park,
it's also worth picking up a detailed
map from the National Trust for
Scotland Ranger Centre.

From the courtyard outside the Arran
Brewery and behind the pink Wineport
Bistro, head up the steps towards the large
brown National Trust for Scotland sign
and enter the rhododendron-studded
woodland beyond. Turn left and follow the
path as it descends to join a larger track
heading west. Ignore the smaller path
branching left and continue along the
main track as it curves right and crosses a
metalled road. Ignore a couple of paths
branching left, then take the next right
turn, signposted 'Hamilton Cemetery'.
This narrower path winds
through more bracken-
covered parkland before
arriving at a small

gated cemetery. Brodick Castle is the ancient seat of the Dukes of Hamilton and this small private graveyard represents the last resting place of the 11th and 12th Dukes and the wife of the latter. Leaving this secluded spot, continue along the path as it traces a wide loop, eventually bearing southeast.

Cross a footbridge, another path and an awkward metal gate before going over another footbridge to emerge alongside a small visitor centre and ranger station with toilets.

After exploring the visitor facilities, follow one of the many paths towards the main castle building and decide whether to enter the castle or simply admire from the outside. With the castle behind, head diagonally right to pick up a path heading west, and follow this as it passes a small information/ticket hut to return to the start of the route.

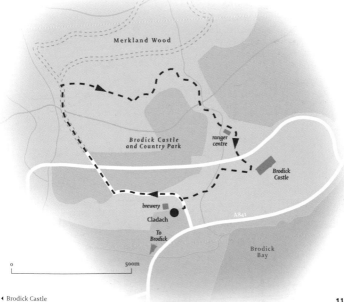

Brodick Standing Stones

Distance 4km **Time** 1 hour 30
Terrain earth paths, surfaced roads and
sandy beach **Map** OS Explorer 361 or
Landranger 69 **Access** Stagecoach bus
(324) to Cladach

**A short, easy walk through woodland,
along estate roads and over the golden
sands of Brodick Bay.**

Cross the road from Cladach Car Park
and head towards the group of buildings
clustered around the Arran Brewery.
Take the uphill path adjacent to the
brewery shop, signposted 'Goatfell', and
enter the woodland. Follow the easy path
for a short distance through the mature
trees before branching left through a
gate signposted 'Easceanoch Trail'. The
path drops downhill to skirt the lower
reaches of the woodland, before curving
right to reach a footbridge over the
Cnocan Burn.

Head left to cross this, then left again
on the far bank. The pleasant path follows
the burn before leaving the woods to
reach the elegant beech-lined access road
for the castle. Turn left and travel a short
distance to reach a series of gaps in the
hedge – step through these to view the
standing stones – one on the left and two
on the right. The craggy grandeur of Glen
Rosa beyond offers a fitting backdrop.
Continue along the road to reach the
castle gates at the A841.

Pass through the gates and turn right
along the busy road – there are no
pavements, so be prepared to use the
grass verges when necessary. Follow the
main road as it crosses the Glenrosa Water
via the Rosa Bridge and turns sharply left
to pass the Isle of Arran Heritage
Museum. Continue on to reach a large
standing stone in the roadside hedge on
the left, followed by Brodick Primary

◄ The golden sands of Brodick Bay

School on the right. Just past the standing stone is a small parking area and bus stance, with a good path leading onto the golf course. Follow this to reach a footbridge back over the Glenrosa Water.

Follow the footpath towards the shore.

This veers left to run between the beach and the greens – it is possible to cross the dunes and walk along the sandy shore if preferred. On reaching the Cnocan Burn, turn inland and cross a footbridge to reach the car park at Cladach.

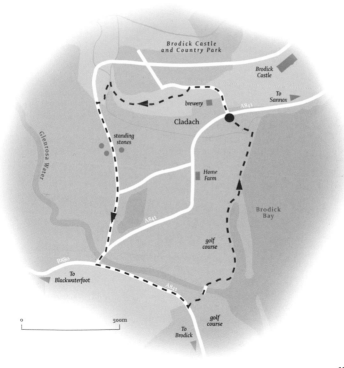

Clauchlands and Corriegills

Distance 11km **Time** 4 hours
Terrain metalled roads and good, clear
tracks, boggy in places **Map** OS Explorer
361 or Landranger 69 **Access** Stagecoach
buses to Brodick Ferry Terminal

**This circuit takes in the low hills south of
Brodick, with panoramic views over the
bays of Brodick and Lamlash.**

From Brodick Pier, pass the tourist
information centre and follow the A841
left uphill, ignoring the left turn
signposted Strathwhillan to take the
following left turn signposted for
Corriegills. As it rises, this minor road
offers views across Brodick Bay to the
Goatfell range beyond. Descending
through the scattered houses of North
and South Corriegills, the surfaced road
finishes at Corriegills Bridge and you turn
left onto a rough vehicle track through a
band of mixed woodland.

This continues to traverse the hillside
before dropping slightly; just before
reaching the last buildings, follow a small
signposted track branching off to the
right. The junction is easy to miss, despite
the signpost – turn around if you've gone
past the buildings. The path crosses a
small burn before diving through
densely-packed forest to emerge on a
rough footpath on a bracken-clad slope
with the rounded profile of Dun Fionn
ahead and the sea below.

Pause at the bench to take in the
panoramic sea views back towards
Goatfell, before heading over the crest of
the hill to be met with equally stunning
views of Lamlash Bay and Holy Isle. Bear
right before the stile and interpretation
board for a steep climb up a grassy trail,
ignoring the path heading left downhill
towards Lamlash. The route is initially
flanked by woodland before opening up

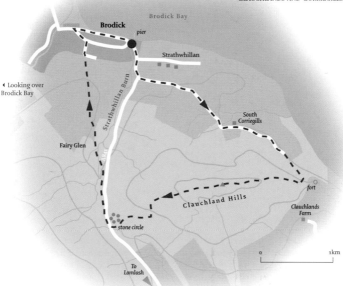

Brodick Bay

Brodick

pier

Strathwhillan

◀ Looking over
Brodick Bay

Strathwhillan Burn

South
Corriegills

Fairy Glen

fort

Clauchland Hills

Clauchlands
Farm

stone circle

0   1km

To
Lamlash

on approach to the crest of the ridge,
with a rollercoaster path undulating to
the large summit cairn of the Clauchland
Hills (259m).

Follow the often boggy path down
heathery slopes, again with views of
Brodick Bay, to a fork. Take either route
through the heather as the paths rejoin
and descend to the wide forest road.
There is the option of turning left here to
view a low mound and partial burial
chamber, a 1.5km detour; otherwise turn
right – enjoying the views to Holy Isle –
towards the A841. On the right just before
you join the road is the stone circle of
Cnoc na Dail, an ancient meeting place for
local crofters.

Cross the road and turn right along a
good path running parallel to it towards
Brodick. This soon reaches a small
Forestry Commission car park with a view
indicator identifying the peaks of
the Goatfell range. Turn left and follow
the path into an area of mature woodland
known as Fairy Glen. Cross two
footbridges on this easy path and go
through a gate before passing straight
through a path junction to carry on
along a surfaced road on the outskirts
of Brodick. Turn left at the junction and
follow the road to emerge on the main
road running along Brodick seafront.
Turn right to return to the ferry terminal.

Glen Rosa

Distance 9.5km **Time** 3 hours
Terrain beaten earth tracks, aggregate
footpaths and surfaced roads; can get
very boggy in places
Map OS Explorer 361 or Landranger 69
Access Stagecoach bus (324) to Cladach

**A circular walk through wonderful
Glen Rosa with views to the craggy
peaks of the Goatfell range.**

From the courtyard of the Arran
Brewery, take the Goatfell path in the far
corner and follow this as it ascends into
the woodland. Take the first turning on
the left, signposted 'Easceanoch Trail', and
accompany this earth track down through
mature woodland to eventually cross a

wooden footbridge. On the far aside,
climb back up to reach a metalled road at
a stone bridge. Don't cross this bridge;
instead go straight ahead, crossing the
road to pick up the 'Cnocan Gorge Trail'.
Ignore the trail leading off to the right
after 50m, as well as the next diversion
towards 'Duchess's Pool', and continue to
climb steadily.

At the next junction, turn left to follow
the 'Glen Rosa' sign along a grassy track
which skirts alongside coniferous forest
with open moorland below and
increasingly dramatic views ahead. The
path reaches a T-junction just before a
drystane dyke; turn right here and pass
through a gap in another dyke to then

turn left. The path through the trees is not well defined – just keep skirting along the edge of the forest to reach a gate. Passing through this takes you out onto the open hillside.

A narrow and often very wet path now traverses the lower slopes of Creag Rosa with the Glenrosa Water below. The views improve as this path leads deeper into the glen, with the A'Chir ridge ahead and Cir Mhor emerging as the route curves northwards. The path eventually descends

to the river and a footbridge. If, after crossing, you want better views of the surrounding peaks, you can carry on up Glen Rosa as far as you like, then retrace your steps.

The return path follows the Glenrosa Water to join a vehicle track and metalled road at rustic Glenrosa Campsite. After 1km, this joins the B880; turn left here and carry on to a junction with the A841. Turn left, cross the Rosa Bridge and follow the road for 1km to reach the start of the route.

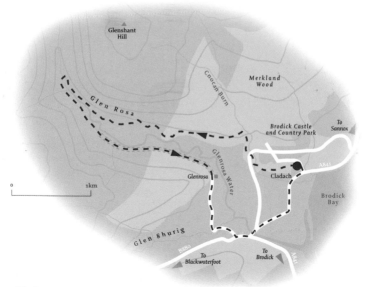

Glen Cloy and Fairy Glen

Distance 10km **Time** 3 hours 30
Terrain earth paths, forestry tracks and
surfaced roads **Map** OS Explorer 361 or
Landranger 69 **Access** Stagecoach buses
to Brodick

**An easy woodland circuit along forestry
roads and good footpaths**.

Head uphill along Alma Road, adjacent
to Brodick Post Office, for 500m and take
the lane signposted 'Lamlash' on the
right. Follow this uphill, ignoring a few
side roads to reach a good earthen path
continuing onwards in a hedge-lined
avenue. The ascent soon eases and the
path enters an area of birch woodland.
Continue into more commercial forestry
and cross a couple of footbridges over
tributaries of the Strathwhillan Burn to
reach a picnic area and car park. Here, a

view indicator identifies the peaks of the
Goatfell range which are laid out on the
horizon. Take the path signposted
'Lamlash' which runs uphill alongside the
A841 to reach a car park located across the
road from the Bronze Age stone circle of
Cnoc na Dail, an ancient meeting place for
local crofters.

Head uphill away from the road along a
good forestry track and take the first right
through the clear-fell. The views across
Brodick Bay and the northern mountains
are superb and the track provides
ample opportunity to enjoy them.
Continue downhill to where a
stand of conifers on the right has
escaped felling; the picnic
bench on a promontory
overlooking Glen Cloy and the
waterfalls cascading down the

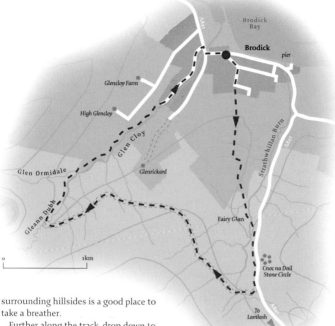

surrounding hillsides is a good place to take a breather.

Further along the track, drop down to cross the footbridge over the burn in Gleann Dubh and climb uphill on the far side, ignoring the path bearing left towards the head of the glen. The earthen footpath leads you above the Glencloy Water to cross a wooden footbridge before continuing to a boggy field. Cross this and the next field via a faint grass path before passing through a gate to reach a vehicle track by a group of buildings.

This track shadows the now more substantial Glencloy Water on the right with grazing land on the left offering

views to Goatfell in the distance. Where the main track turns left towards High Glencloy, keep to the right instead to continue alongside the river by way of a well-made footpath. Pass the holiday chalets of the Auchrannie Resort on the left and, later, a group of industrial units to reach the A841 at Cloy Bridge. Turn right and follow the pavement past sports fields and the war memorial to reach the post office on the right.

◀ Entering the woods of Gleann Dubh

19

Three Beinns Horseshoe

Distance 14.5km **Time** 6 hours 30
Terrain rough bouldery paths, boggy in
Coire a'Bhradain; starts and ends on a
good track through Glen Rosa
Map OS Explorer 361 or Landranger 69
Access Stagecoach buses (322, 324) to the
end of the road into Glen Rosa

A demanding horseshoe circuit of the
high mountains encircling the bleak
moorland of Coire a'Bhradain above
Glen Rosa.

Head into Glen Rosa from the campsite
at the end of the surfaced road. There is
little parking here, so an approach via
public transport is recommended.
Continue along the track with views of
Goatfell to the right joined with angular
Cir Mhòr via The Saddle at the head of the
glen, and the Witch's Step above Glen
Sannox beyond. Cross the footbridge over
the Garbh Allt and turn immediately left
up a rocky path running parallel to the

burn. Pass through a kissing gate to reach
the wide tussocky expanse of Coire
a'Bhradain with the full horseshoe ridge
in view ahead.

The rough path has the potential to be
boggy and occasionally braided as walkers
forge their own way through the terrain.
Enter another fenced enclosure – erected
to help the reintroduction of native
woodland in the steep gorge – and look
out for a steep narrow path leading to a
ford across the burn. Scramble up the far
side and head for the kissing gate in the
fence to begin a gentle ascent of the
moorland. This gives way to a more
challenging path threading around and
over the boulders and slabs towards the
summit of Beinn Nuis.

Before reaching the summit you can
make a short detour west (at around the
700m contour) to find the ruins of the
B-24D Liberator that crashed into the
hillside on 20th August 1943 with

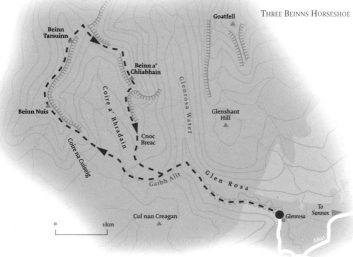

Goatfell

Beinn
Tarsuinn

Beinn a'
Chliabhain

Glenrosa Water

Glenshant
Hill

Beinn Nuis

Coire a' Bhradain

Coire na Cuileag

Cnoc
Breac

Garbh Allt

Glen Rosa

Cul nan Creagan

Glenrosa

To
Sannox

0   1km

the loss of all ten personnel onboard. Regain the rocky ridge on an obvious path, occasionally bearing left to avoid some scrambling over the rocky outcrops. Just before the final ascent to the summit of Beinn Tarsuinn, look out for the Old Man of Tarsuinn on the right – an outcrop naturally sculpted into a human profile and appearing to look out to the sea over Brodick.

Continue onwards to the twin summits of the second Beinn – Tarsuinn – with panoramic views in all directions. The steep descent to Bealach an Fhir-bhogha is far from easy, with a certain amount of scrambling and negotiation of substantial boulders. A worn path is occasionally visible, but as much of the route involves rock slabs it's best to pick the path that appears most sensible. From the bealach, turn right and drop downhill, again along

a steep, narrow path, to arrive on the ridge above Coire Daingean with Beinn a'Chliabhain ahead. Follow the path along the grassy ridge, before forking left for the summit. (A clearer path bearing right traverses well below the summit, so don't miss the turning to reach the top.)

A minimal ascent is rewarded with a grassy summit ridge punctuated by rocky slabs which make ideal picnic tables. Carry on along the ridge path to rejoin the alternative path and begin the descent into Coire a'Bhradain. Pass the cairn on Cnoc Breac as the gradient eases and the path crosses the moorland again. Rejoin the outward path at the kissing gate above the Garbh Allt and drop downhill alongside the tumbling waterfalls to emerge on the familiar track in Glen Rosa. Turn right to return to the campsite.

Goatfell from Brodick Castle

Distance 10.5km Time 6 hours
Terrain beaten earth tracks, aggregate
footpaths and some light scrambling
over granite boulders below the summit
Map OS Explorer 361 or Landranger 69
Access Stagecoach bus (324) to Cladach

The most popular route up Goatfell, the
highest point in Arran. The route begins
from the Cladach Visitor Centre: take the
Fisherman's Walk from Brodick to the
start point if coming directly from the
ferry pier (see page 8).

From the courtyard outside the Arran
Brewery, take the Goatfell path in the far
corner and follow this as it ascends into
the woodland. Ignore the paths branching
off, first to the right and then the left, and
go straight across the metalled road.
Ignore the next minor path that intersects,

and the subsequent paths joining from
the left and right. Eventually, the main
path curves sharply right; carry straight on
as the way gets rougher.

There are now no further navigation
difficulties, though the walking will
become somewhat harder. The path
leaves the woodland to cross heather
moorland accompanied by the various
tributaries of the Cnocan Burn which
tumble over a series of small waterfalls
towards their eventual discharge in
Brodick Bay – looking behind, this comes
into view as the path ascends. Cross a
footbridge at Mill Burn before the
gradient increases to reach the ridge
between Meall Breac and Goatfell.

Turn left and follow one of the routes
over and between the large rocks towards
the summit – tantalisingly close for this

◄ Ascending Goatfell

final section of the route. Perseverance is rewarded with spectacular views over the surrounding ridges and peaks, across the Clyde Estuary and to Ireland on a clear day. Return via the same route – enjoying the panoramic views over Brodick Bay – or descend to Corrie and return to the start point via the regular bus service.

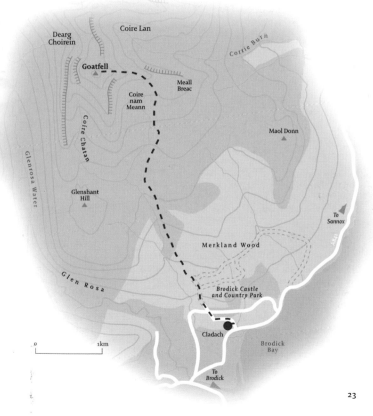

Lamlash to Brodick

Distance 6km **Time** 3 hours
Terrain metalled roads and good,
clear paths **Map** OS Explorer 361 or
Landranger 69 **Access** Stagecoach bus
(323) to Lamlash from Brodick

**Catch the bus from Brodick to return by
this linear walk running parallel to the
main road but maintaining a safe and
pleasant distance, thanks to purpose-
built paths and an old track through the
wooded Fairy Glen.**

From the seafront in Lamlash, look for
the signs for Brodick and head northeast,
following the main road as it curves left

and climbs uphill. The pavement ends
outside the Lamlash Golf Club, but is
quickly replaced by a good path running
parallel to the road. Follow this as it
crosses a footbridge before veering
slightly away from the road and into
the forest.

After 1.5km you come to a small car park
– you can cross the main road here and
view the ancient stone circle of Cnoc na
Dail where crofters once met to discuss
local issues. Cross back over the road and
turn right along the footpath. You soon
reach a Forestry Commission car park
with a view indicator identifying the

peaks of the Goatfell range. Turn left and
follow the path into an area of mature
woodland known as Fairy Glen. Cross two
footbridges on this easy path and go

through a gate before passing straight
across a path junction to arrive on a
surfaced road on the outskirts of Brodick.

Turn left at the junction and carry on to
emerge on the main road running along
Brodick seafront. Turn right to return to
the ferry terminal.

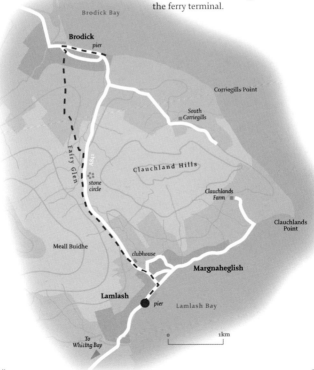

Clauchlands Point and Dun Fionn

Distance 5km **Time** 2 hours
Terrain earth and grass paths and
surfaced roads; not recommended for a
windy day **Map** OS Explorer 361 or
Landranger 69 **Access** Stagecoach bus
(323) to Lamlash

**A circuit featuring coastal walking and
an iron age fort with a pleasant return
through farm and woodland.**

This walk begins at the car park on the
shore road from Lamlash to Clauchlands
Farm. Go through the gate to continue
along the coast towards Clauchlands Point
and the tiny Hamilton Isle. On the point,
there are three paths: ignore the wide track
heading inland and the signed Coastal Way
ahead to follow a faint path between the

two, which climbs steeply to a pillbox. An
obvious position for such a fortification,
the views across Lamlash Bay to Holy Isle
are tremendous. The bay is Scotland's first
No Take Zone (NTZ): 'an area of sea and
seabed from which no marine life can be
removed by any fishing method, whether
recreational or commercial'.

Follow a narrow grassy path along the
top of the cliffs, remaining seaward of the
fence and ancient drystane dyke. As the
gap between fence and cliff narrows, it
becomes obvious why this walk is not
suitable for a blustery day; continue with
caution and enjoy the views across to the
Ayrshire coastline. After 1km, the path
rises steeply inland up the rocky natural
ramparts of Dun Fionn to reach the

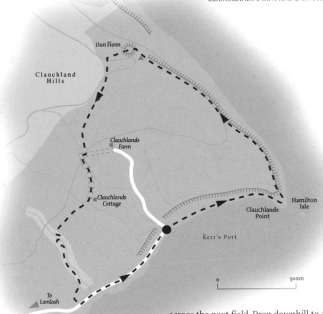

summit trig point. Pause for a while to enjoy the views before dropping downhill on the inland side of the mound to a path junction. Turn right to reach Brodick via Corriegills or turn left along a grassy path to complete the circuit.

The path leads downhill towards Lamlash Bay, with Holy Isle a constant companion, to reach a field beyond a kissing gate. Head diagonally right along a faint path towards a gap in the boundary hedge; cross the footbridge and follow the marker posts left, then right

across the next field. Drop downhill to a stile in the far right corner of the field, crossing this and heading right along the farm access track. This curves left, then right at Clauchlands Cottage, climbing briefly before descending once again towards a wooded burn.

Look out for a stile on the left and go over this to descend to a small ford where stepping stones aid your crossing. Follow the path to the left on the far side. Emerging at a surfaced road alongside the self-catering cottages at Prospect Hill, continue downhill to reach the shore road. Turn left for the car park or right for Lamlash.

◀ The clifftop path to Dun Fionn

Urie Loch Hill Trail

Distance 6km **Time** 3 hours 30 (return)
Terrain footpaths, often muddy in places;
very short section of loose rock
Map OS Explorer 361 or Landranger 69
Access Stagecoach bus (323) to the start
of the Ross Road south of Lamlash

A tough, steep walk to a remote loch
set in quiet moorland. Birdwatchers
should make space in their bag for a
pair of binoculars.

Start from Dyemill car park, off the Ross
Road. Cross the bridge and almost
immediately turn right to access a well-
made footpath through the trees,
signposted 'Urie Loch'. Cross a footbridge
to accompany the path as it shadows the
fast-flowing burn. Ignore the next
footbridge on the left for now, and climb
uphill past a small bench. The path runs
uphill through clear-felled forest for some
distance with the views over Lamlash and
Holy Isle improving as you gain height.

Eventually, the path re-enters the

forestry and becomes wet underfoot.
Thankfully, this is a popular route so the
deep footprints highlighting the
misfortunes of others indicate the bits to
avoid. If attempting this route in July, the
path may well be clogged with cross-
country runners slipping and sliding
through the mud as part of the Urie Loch
Hill Race. The current record holder
managed the return trip in under 45
minutes – an impressive achievement.

The wide forest ride steepens before
levelling out at a series of clearings
– a welcome break from both the
relentless gradient and the shade of
the forest canopy.

Where the forest ride finally runs out
beneath the oppressive Creag na h-Ennie
at the 300m contour, the path takes a less
direct route – contouring left to avoid the
steep hillside. Remaining above the
treeline, there is a very short rocky
scramble before the path reaches the
heather-clad moorland. A white marker

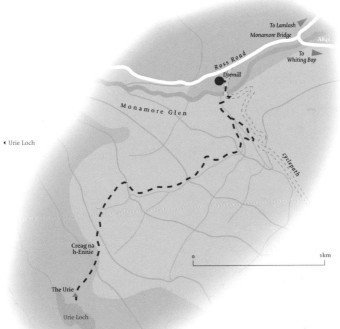

◄ Urie Loch

post indicates the correct route onwards (though the path is fairly obvious); follow this to reach the summit of The Urie at 425m, with Urie Loch at the end of a narrow (and wet) path below.

The small grass-covered island in the loch is in fact man-made to encourage red-throated divers to nest. If the weather is favourable then a rocky outcrop provides a great spot to rest and observe the wildlife. Watch out for a glimpse of the rare hen harrier hunting over the expansive heather moorland.

Return by the same route until you reach the footbridge by the bench. Cross this and take the left fork to follow the burn down towards the car park. The adjacent flat grassy area is equipped with tables and benches – a good spot for a picnic to celebrate your ascent, even if it wasn't achieved in record-breaking time.

Holy Isle

**Distance 7.3km Time 3 hours 30
Terrain rough footpaths and some
scrambling over rocks below the summit
of Mullach Mòr Map OS Explorer 361 or
Landranger 69 Access Stagecoach bus
(323) to Lamlash and passenger ferry
from Lamlash Pier**

**A fairly tough walk to the highest point
on Holy Isle in Lamlash Bay, returning by
the easy shoreline path.**

Holy Isle is around 3km long and 1km
wide and is dominated by the rocky
Mullach Mòr (314m). The island was home
to 6th-century hermit monk Saint Molaise
who spent 20 years living in a cave here,
giving the island the old Gaelic name of
Eilean MoLaise. From Lamlash, the ferry
crosses in summer months, subject to
tide and weather, and infrequently during
spring and autumn. Winter crossings are
by arrangement only.

The island is now owned by the Samyé

Ling Buddhist Community who have
established the Centre for World Peace
and Health on the north of the island.
Coming off the ferry, passengers are
generally met by one of the community
volunteers who will explain the non-
onerous island rules.

From the jetty, turn left and cross the
foreshore to pass through a flagged gap in
the drystane dyke and head uphill. Hug
the field boundary on the left to reach a
stile and bright red sign pointing 'To the
Top'. Cross the stile and climb the
pleasant path through native woodland
and bracken to reach another stile with
heather moorland beyond. Over the stile
watch out for the rare breeds that inhabit
the island, protected by the nature reserve
to the east. As the path winds through the
heather, wild Eriskay ponies, bearded
Saanen goat and Soay sheep can be
glimpsed – these should be observed
from afar and not fed.

◀ A rock painting on Holy Isle

The moorland path is fairly rough, maintaining a steep gradient until just below the summit of Mullach Beag. At this point, the path becomes rockier and the surrounding heather is punctuated by large boulders. The views open up as the ridge path continues towards Mullach Mòr. It then drops to a col, which marks the start of a steep, rough scramble to gain the highest point on the island.

On the descent, care needs to be taken to avoid the cliffs on either side. The path also runs through heather which conceals nasty crevasses. Respect the roped-off areas and remain on the obvious path which gently slopes down Creag Liath to a junction. Turn left to view Pillar Rock Lighthouse – the first square lighthouse built by the famous Stevenson family. Return to the path junction and bear southwest towards the inner lighthouse facing Arran, again built by a Stevenson and known locally as Wee Donald. The buildings here are inhabited by a community of nuns who are undertaking four-year retreats. Follow the path below the home of Lama Yeshe Losal Rinpoche and curve northwest to follow the western shoreline.

The grassy path passes below a series of colourful Buddhist paintings on the rocks depicting different deities and teachers of the Kagyu Lineage of Tibetan Buddhism.

Halfway along the path is Holy Well, an historic water source that sadly does not to meet EU standards for drinking water. Shortly after the well, a sign indicates steps up to the cave inhabited by Saint Molaise – the walls and ceiling are adorned with Norse runes, consisting mainly of personal names but also an unusually designed cross.

The path continues along the shore to reach The Boathouse, an information centre staffed by community volunteers where a cup of tea or coffee will often be offered while you wait for the return ferry.

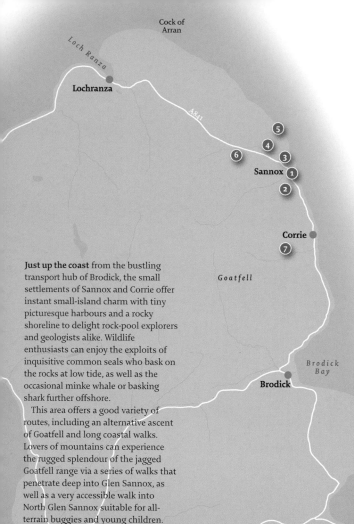

Cock of Arran

Loch Ranza

Lochranza

A841

⑤
④
③
⑥
Sannox ①
②

Corrie
⑦

Goatfell

Just up the coast from the bustling transport hub of Brodick, the small settlements of Sannox and Corrie offer instant small-island charm with tiny picturesque harbours and a rocky shoreline to delight rock-pool explorers and geologists alike. Wildlife enthusiasts can enjoy the exploits of inquisitive common seals who bask on the rocks at low tide, as well as the occasional minke whale or basking shark further offshore.

This area offers a good variety of routes, including an alternative ascent of Goatfell and long coastal walks. Lovers of mountains can experience the rugged splendour of the jagged Goatfell range via a series of walks that penetrate deep into Glen Sannox, as well as a very accessible walk into North Glen Sannox suitable for all-terrain buggies and young children.

Brodick Bay

Brodick

Sannox, Corrie and the Northern Hills

Glen Sannox

Distance 2.5km **Time** 1 hour
Terrain metalled road and good
aggregate footpaths, rougher further up
the glen; large stepping stones across
Sannox Burn **Map** OS Explorer 361 or
Landranger 69 **Access** Stagecoach bus
(324) to Sannox

**A short walk around the foot of dramatic
Glen Sannox with an option to go further
into this rugged mountain environment.**

Sannox is located around 12km north of
Brodick on the A841 and is easily reached
by a bus which will drop and collect you
at the car park next to the telephone box.
From the car park, cross the A841 and
head up the road between a postbox and

white Glen Cottage, conveniently
signposted 'Glen Sannox'. Go through a
kissing gate and follow the track as it
passes a walled cemetery on the left.

The path soon becomes unsurfaced, but
is good quality nonetheless, and swings
right before passing through another
gate. A tall navigation mast will come into
view ahead – this is one of a set of leading
lights used by vessels in the Firth of Clyde
to indicate a measured mile, and hence
calculate the top speed of new Clyde-built
ships. The lower mast can be seen on the
way to North Sannox (*see page 38*) and the

rest of the set that make up the mile on the Cock of Arran walk (*see page 42*).

The path rises gently before curving left, offering views of rugged Caisteal Abhail, a key feature in the 'Sleeping Warrior' profile of the north Arran hills as seen from the Ayrshire coast. As the path reaches the beginning of a line of beech trees, leave it by turning right and descending to a footbridge across the Sannox Burn. Cross and turn immediately left, ignoring other paths branching off in several directions.

This clear path, rough in places, follows the course of the river up the glen, passing the remains of the baryte mines that were in operation in Glen Sannox well into the 20th century. Keep an eye out for a set of stepping stones crossing the river off the main path. At this point there are two options – either continue deeper into the glen for increasingly panoramic views of mountain scenery which includes Cir Mhor and The Saddle, or cross the burn and follow the path back past the line of beech trees.

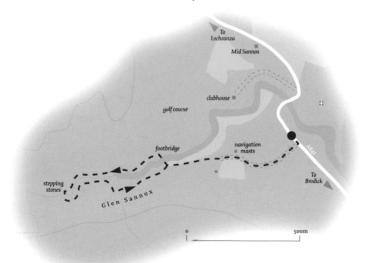

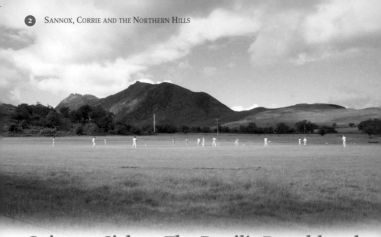

Coire na Ciche – The Devil's Punchbowl

Distance 6km **Time** 3 hours
Terrain obvious but often boggy paths,
apart from the last pathless stretch into
the corrie **Map** OS Explorer 361 or
Landranger 69 **Access** Stagecoach bus
(324) to North Sannox

**A straightforward but strenuous linear
walk into the secluded corrie of The
Devil's Punchbowl below the steep
mountain of Cioch na h-Oighe.**

Sannox is around 12km north of Brodick
on the A841. The route starts from the car
park next to a telephone box, and can be
easily reached by bus which will drop and
collect you at the large bus shelter. From
here, cross the A841 and head up the road
between a postbox and white Glen
Cottage, signposted 'Glen Sannox'. Go
through a kissing gate and follow the
track as it passes a walled cemetery.

The path soon becomes unsurfaced but

good quality nonetheless, and swings
right before passing through another
gate. A tall white navigation mast will
come into view ahead – this is one of a set
of leading lights used by vessels in the
Firth of Clyde to indicate a measured mile.

The path rises gently before curving left,
offering views of the rugged Caisteal
Abhail, a key feature in the 'Sleeping
Warrior' profile of the north Arran hills as
seen from the Ayrshire coast. As the path
reaches the beginning of a line of beech
trees, ignore the path dropping right to
the Sannox Burn and push on into the
glen past ruined mine workings. The path
soon reaches the waters of the Allt a'
Chapuill; don't cross this, take a narrow
path running up the left bank instead.

Narrow and overgrown but reasonably
easy to navigate, the path winds past
mossy boulders and twisted trees
alongside the tumbling burn. A fenced

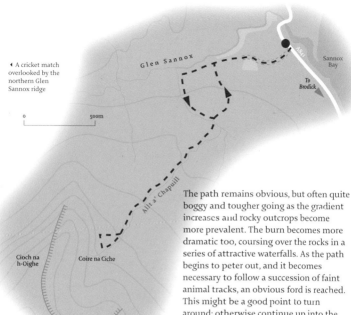

◄ A cricket match overlooked by the northern Glen Sannox ridge

Glen Sannox

Sannox Bay

To Brodick

0   500m

Allt a' Chapuill

Cioch na h-Oighe

Coire na Ciche

The path remains obvious, but often quite boggy and tougher going as the gradient increases and rocky outcrops become more prevalent. The burn becomes more dramatic too, coursing over the rocks in a series of attractive waterfalls. As the path begins to peter out, and it becomes necessary to follow a succession of faint animal tracks, an obvious ford is reached. This might be a good point to turn around; otherwise continue up into the corrie on the pathless terrain.

There are many interesting rock formations directly below the steep slopes of Cioch na h-Oighe, providing good seats from which to enjoy the sweeping views across the Firth of Clyde and the mainland. Retrace your steps to the lower ford across the Allt a'Chapuill and take the path straight ahead rather than turning left on the far side. This leads across farmland before meeting an ATV track joining from the left. Follow this back to the Glen Sannox path and turn right to return to the car park.

enclosure on the left contains a deep shaft associated with a barytes (barium sulphate) mine that operated in the glen until the late 1930s. As the path rises, the burn remains at the bottom of a deep gorge. Eventually, both meet at a suitable crossing point.

On the far side of the water, the path forks almost immediately – take the left fork over open ground to reach the Allt a' Chapuill again, and follow it upstream.

North Sannox by the Coastal Way

Distance 3.5km **Time** 1 hour 30 (return)
Terrain good aggregate footpaths and
sandy tracks; large stepping stones
across Sannox Burn **Map** OS Explorer 361
or Landranger 69 **Access** Stagecoach bus
(324) to Sannox

This short linear walk along the coast to
North Sannox provides an easy link to
further walks on this section of the
Arran Coastal Way.

   Sannox is located around 12km north of
Brodick on the A841 – the route starts
from a car park next to a telephone box,
and can easily be reached by bus which
will drop and collect you at the large bus
shelter in the car park. From here, follow

the waymarked route to the north of the
car park to cross a large set of concrete
stepping stones. Turn right along the path
on the far bank to head slightly uphill,
shadowing the Sannox Burn before
turning left towards a sandy beach.

   Passing a couple of houses on the left,
the path also leads past a large white
navigation mast, one of a set of leading
lights used by vessels in the Firth of Clyde
to indicate a measured mile and hence
calculate the top speed of new Clyde-built
ships. The upper masts can be seen on the
Glen Sannox walk (*see page 34*), and the
rest of the set that make up the mile on
the Cock of Arran walk (*see page 42*).

   The path leaves the shore at this point

and curves inland beneath a dramatic cliff face before returning to the coast with views across the Firth to Bute and Ayrshire. Remain on the path until it reaches the North Sannox Burn, turning left onto a clear aggregate path through the woods alongside the fast-flowing river before it emerges at a surfaced road. Either retrace your steps from this point or head right over the bridge to reach another car park and the beginning of the Cock of Arran walk after 1km.

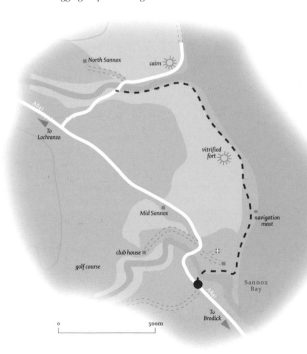

◀ Royal Navy ship on manoeuvres in the Sound of Bute

North Sannox Wood

Distance 4km **Time** 2 hours
Terrain rough earth footpaths, boggy in
places **Map** OS Explorer 361 or
Landranger 69 **Access** Stagecoach bus
(324) to North Sannox

**A walk through the forest to a trig
point with superb views over the
Sannox mountains.**

This walk begins at a car park and picnic
site on the coast alongside the North
Sannox Burn, and can be reached via a
pleasant walk from Sannox, as well as by
car or bus along the A841. An interpretive
board describes variations of this walk –
which begins via the gate at the edge of
the forest.

Climb uphill through the conifer
plantation to a fork in the path with four
colour-coded walks indicated on a

waymarker post. This route follows the
yellow route, so bear left. The broad easy
path soon reaches a clearing with a picnic
bench offering the first glimpse of the
angular Sannox peaks – these views
improve as the walk progresses. Ignore a
path heading right (the red route) to
continue through a boggy patch. Further
clearings offer tantalising previews of the
vistas to be experienced at the summit.
The green route peels off to the right if a
shorter walk is preferred.

The path now enters a wide forest ride
flanked by heather and bracken, leading
past a tall white navigation beacon – one
of a set of leading lights used by vessels
in the Firth of Clyde to indicate a
measured mile and hence calculate the
top speed of new Clyde-built ships. Just
past this, the path splits; head left and

◀ Entering North Sannox Wood

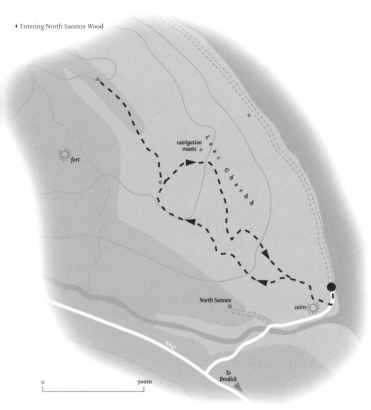

navigation masts

L e a c   G h a r b h

fort

North Sannox

cairn

A841

To Brodick

0   500m

continue through the trees to reach an open area of moorland with the path clearly signposted. Trending left, the path continues to rise through bracken to reach a trig point on top of a rocky outcrop. The views from here are a great reward for the relentless climb, so a

lingering break is highly recommended.

Return to the path split by the navigation beacon, this time turning left to continue along the forest ride. From here, the way is marked with blue arrows for a slightly different return route enclosed by tall conifers.

Cock of Arran and the Fallen Rocks

Distance 12.5km **Time** 4 hours (one way)
Terrain clear grassy tracks interspersed
with rough, boggy paths and some areas
of easy scrambling over boulders
Map OS Explorer 361 or Landranger 69
Access Stagecoach bus (324) to
North Sannox

An enjoyable coastal walk through a
landscape of particular interest to fans
of geology and its history.

Head onto the clear coastal path from
the car park at Sannox Bay and pass
through a gate with the notice 'Fallen
Rocks 1½ miles'. The path is easy and
trouble free as it runs alongside the forest
on what was once the beach before the
end of the Ice Age allowed Arran to
'rebound' upwards as the weight of ice

abated. Pass a tall white navigation mast –
one of a set of leading lights used by
vessels in the Firth of Clyde to indicate a
measured mile and hence calculate the
top speed of new Clyde-built ships.

Passing the edge of the forest, the path
weaves easily through the 'Fallen Rocks', a
slight understatement given the size of
the huge conglomerate boulders
stretching from the cliffs to the sea.
Continue as a narrower path leads past a
series of small caves, one large enough to
sleep in, and becomes quite waterlogged
and boggy in places.

Eventually, you come to Laggan
Cottage; overlooking the Firth of Clyde,
with Bute, the Cumbraes and Ayrshire
beyond, it is a good spot for lunch. The
route continues as an obvious path, past

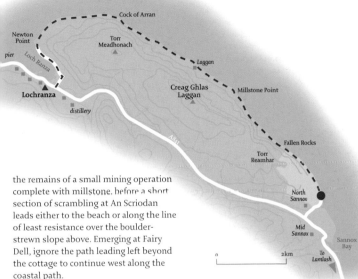

the remains of a small mining operation complete with millstone, before a short section of scrambling at An Scriodan leads either to the beach or along the line of least resistance over the boulder-strewn slope above. Emerging at Fairy Dell, ignore the path leading left beyond the cottage to continue west along the coastal path.

The path becomes easier, passing further fascinating rock formations along the seashore, including Hutton's Unconformity, one of the sites at which geologist James Hutton (1726-1797) first identified the geological feature that was to lead to the notion that the Earth's surface has evolved over an immense period of time. At a junction, follow the right-hand path as it skirts alongside the shore, passing rocky outcrops harvested for their shellfish by locals who venture out at low tide.

As you curve gently around the headland of Newton Point, the straggling settlement of Lochranza comes into view, cradled by hills with the castle standing sentinel over the yacht moorings in the bay. Carry on as the track becomes a metalled road and leads into the town itself. There is a bus stop at the ferry slip for the return to the start of the walk; Arran's only youth hostel is in Lochranza if you plan to stay awhile or if you have missed the last bus.

◀ A raised beach overlooking the Firth of Clyde

43

North Glen Sannox

Distance 5.5km **Time** 2 hours
Terrain well-made aggregate paths;
rougher ground further up the glen
Map OS Explorer 361 or Landranger 69
Access Stagecoach bus (324) to car park
by North Sannox Bridge

**An accessible walk on well-made paths
permitting easy access to North Glen
Sannox and its dramatic views.**

Start from the car park off the A841 by
North Sannox Bridge. Before heading off
along the obvious path, spend some time
admiring the view from the bridge – rocky
North Sannox Burn is truly beautiful from
this angle. The Highland Boundary Fault

crosses perpendicular to the A841 around
500m south of the car park, making this
area popular with geologists keen to
study the volcanic rock formations that
make up the Highland Border Complex.
The North Sannox Burn cuts through the
various rock layers that make up this
collision of tectonic plates, offering access
to extruded layers of lava sandwiched
between the black shale and sandstones.

Follow the well-surfaced path leading
into the forest from the far right corner
of the car park – the going is particularly
easy – and keep right as the path forks by
a footbridge. The path over the bridge
leads to a well-placed bench and ideal

◀ North Glen Sannox

spot for lunch, but for the time being ignore this and press on.

Soon entering the forest, the way is flanked by heather and fragrant bog myrtle as the burn begins to drop down into a steep gorge. Step over a couple of tributaries or take the bridge and head deeper into the glen. The first of a series of attractive waterfalls will draw the eye as the gorge becomes narrower and deeper, in places forcing the water into an almost corkscrew effect.

The views open out as you emerge at the edge of the forest, with the jagged

Glen Sannox ridge in view ahead. The distinctive cleft that forms Ceum na Caillich (Witch's Step) is obvious, as well as the castellations of Caisteal Abhail. Eventually, the good path ends at a fence and onward progress is via a rougher, rockier path. The extra effort is rewarded by increasingly dramatic waterfalls and panoramic views into Coire nan Ceum. This rougher path finally peters out and, unless continuing to summit Caisteal Abhail by way of the Carn Mór ridge, it is best from here to retrace your steps to the bench passed earlier or the car park.

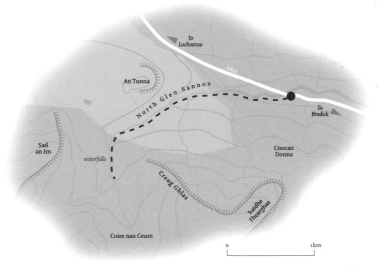

Goatfell from Corrie

Distance 8.5km **Time** 5 hours 30
Terrain a short section of metalled road,
rocky aggregate footpaths and some
light scrambling over granite boulders
below the summit **Map** OS Explorer 361
or Landranger 69 **Access** Stagecoach bus
(324) to Corrie

**Take the less-travelled route to the
summit of Arran's highest peak on
rough but obvious paths.**

From the bus stop in Corrie, head south
along the A841 until you see the sign for
Goatfell off to the right. Follow this to a
junction and take the left-hand fork to
pass a seriously distressed tree stump
overshadowing a painted wooden sign
for Goatfell. Carry on as the metalled
road turns into an aggregate track. Watch
out for the signposted junction indicating
a smaller track to the right which you
accompany until it exits the woodland at
a deer gate. A high fence extends around
the north of the island containing the
large red deer population. Deerstalking is
a significant source of income for the
island and during the autumn season the
hills reverberate with the sound of
gunshots.

Beyond the gate is a well-maintained
but rough path running above the Corrie
Burn and associated waterfalls. Take this,

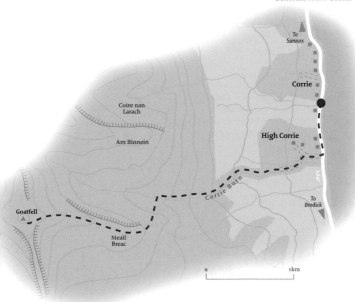

watching for a ford across the river as it narrows – level with the eastern extremity of Meall Breac. The crossing takes you onto a path to gain the ridge. Negotiate the obvious paths through the boulders – you may need to use your hands in places – until you reach the junction with the 'tourist route' from Brodick. Continue straight ahead with the summit firmly in sight, and begin the steep final ascent.

Perseverance is rewarded with a summit adorned with a trig point and view indicator supplementing the spectacular views over the surrounding ridges and peaks, down to Brodick and across the Clyde Estuary to the mainland. On a clear

day, Ireland can be seen on the horizon. At 874m (2866ft) Goatfell summit is the highest point on the island and one of four Corbetts – peaks in Scotland that are between 2500 and 3000ft (762 and 914.4m) high with a relative height of at least 500 feet (152.4m). In summer, a steady stream of Corbett-baggers can be observed ascending Goatfell via the Brodick route, making the ascent from Corrie a quieter (but shorter and steeper) alternative.

Return via the same route – enjoying the panoramic views over the Clyde Estuary – or descend to Brodick (*see page 22*) and return to the start point in Corrie via the regular bus service.

◀ Looking to Corrie from below Goatfell summit

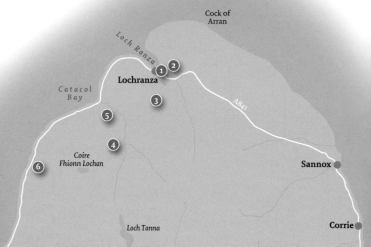

Cock of Arran

Loch Ranza

Lochranza

Catacol Bay

A841

Coire Fhionn Lochan

Sannox

Loch Tanna

Corrie

Brod Ba

Brodick

Lochranza is the most northerly of Arran's villages and home to the island's less known second ferry port conveying passengers and vehicles to Kintyre. Lochranza is also home to Arran Distillery, located to take advantage of the purest water in Scotland (as certified by the Geology Department of Glasgow University no less).

The atmospheric ruins of Lochranza Castle – on which the castle in the Tintin adventure *The Black Island* is said to be based – stands in dramatic isolation on a shingle spit jutting into Loch Ranza, with a healthy population of red deer roaming free over the golf course and frequent visitations from the golden eagles nested on the surrounding mountains. Around Newton Point lies Hutton's Unconformity, where the 'father of modern geology' James Hutton found his first example of an

angular unconformity during a visit in the 18th century.

Further round the coast, Catacol is characterised by a row of cottages known as the Twelve Apostles, built to house those displaced from Gleann Diomhan and the surrounding countryside in the Clearances. Each cottage has a differently-shaped upper window to allow signals from shore to be identified by the fishermen out in the Firth of Clyde.

Loch na Davie ▶

Around Lochranza and Catacol

Fairy Dell

Distance 6km Time 2 hours
Terrain **surfaced and unsurfaced road, grassy tracks and aggregate footpath**
Map **OS Explorer 361 or Landranger 69**
Access **Stagecoach bus (324) to Lochranza**

A popular circuit around the headland north of Loch Ranza to the white cottage at Fairy Dell, said by some to be a gateway to the land of the fairies.

The bus will stop outside the field study centre and church in Lochranza. From here, take the minor road around the north side of the loch, signposted 'Fairy Dell 1½ miles'. This quiet road leads past the golf course and bears left to shadow the shoreline, a place favoured by Loch Ranza's resident seal population – often seen basking on the rocks here.

After passing a few houses and a rough path leading uphill to Whin Cottage, the surfaced road peters out to be replaced by a good footpath leading to a viewpoint and direction indicator.

Rounding Newton Point, the path splits, giving you a boggy inland option or a more pleasant trail hugging the rocky shoreline. The shoreline route offers the opportunity to view Hutton's Unconformity – one of the sites at which geologist James Hutton (1726-1797) first identified the geological feature that was to lead to the notion that Earth's surface has evolved over an immense period of time. Rejoining the inland path at a modern stone circle, continue around the headland beneath the red sandstone cliffs characteristic of this shoreline to reach

◄ Views over the Sound of Bute

the whitewashed cottage at Fairy Dell.

Immediately before a ruined drystane dyke, turn inland into a small patch of woodland alongside the Allt Mòr. Follow the path as it bears right and continues to ascend. After passing a bench with views to Kintyre, Bute and Cowal, the path reaches a couple of houses at the end of a rough track. Take this to reach Whin Cottage, home of the Arran Stonemen who create and sell products made of rock collected locally. The track continues downhill to rejoin the public road on the north shore of the loch.

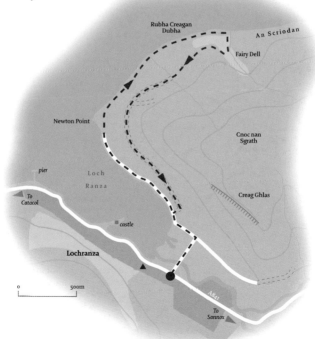

Laggan Cottage from Lochranza

Distance 10km **Time** 3 hours 30
Terrain rough bouldery paths and a short section of quiet road walking
Map OS Explorer 361 or Landranger 69
Access Stagecoach bus (324) to Lochranza

A short but steep route with stunning views across the Clyde Islands.

The bus will stop outside the field study centre and church in Lochranza. Take the minor road opposite, signposted 'Laggan 4 miles'. The quiet road leads past the golf course and bears right – follow this uphill past a succession of houses with views across the glen to rugged Creag a'Chaise and Torr Nead an Eoin. After 1km leave the road by a grassy path, forking left adjacent to an interpretation board. This path is the historic route to Cock Farm from the village and begins a gentle ascent through the grazing land of Glen Chalmadale.

There is never any doubt as to the correct route, so enjoy the unfolding views along the glen to the Witch's Step (Ceum na Caillich) and Caisteal Abhail of North Glen Sannox as the immediate terrain changes from lush farmland to rough heather moorland. Cross a footbridge over pretty Allt Eadaraidh and continue until the path levels out at the pass of Bearradh Tom a'Muidhe at 263m. The views from this point are stunning, with the small island of Inchmarnock in the foreground overshadowed by Bute and the Cowal Peninsula.

The path bears right to reveal ruined Cock Farm far below. The area between Laggan Cottage and Cock Farm was once home to more than 100 people – hence

◄ The Arran Distillery in Glen Chalmadale

the substantial path over the pass – but now lies deserted. Malcolm Macmillan, the grandfather of Daniel Macmillan of Macmillan Publishing fame was born on Cock Farm in 1735. His son, Maurice Crawford Macmillan married Helen (Nellie) Artie Tarleton Belles, and their son Harold became British Prime Minister in 1957. Cock Farm was abandoned in 1912 and now lies empty at the end of a grass track dropping steeply to the left.

Follow the main path as it contours below the crags of Creag Ghlas Laggan before descending more directly to whitewashed Laggan Cottage above a rocky shoreline. From this point, it is possible to return to Lochranza via the Cock of Arran (*see page 42*) to create a pleasant circuit, or simply retrace your steps up and over the pass.

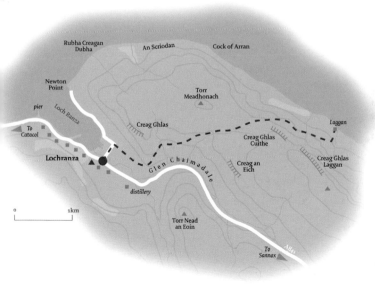

Loch na Davie loop

Distance 17km Time 5 hours 30 Terrain rough bouldery paths, very boggy in places; starts and ends with a section of quiet road walking Map OS Explorer 361 or Landranger 69 Access Stagecoach bus (324) to Lochranza

A rough and wild circuit through glens and over passes to reach remote Loch na Davie, reputedly the source of the purest water in Scotland.

From Lochranza, head south along the quiet A841 to pass the ruined castle standing proudly on a promontory. Whilst the majority of the visible remains are from the 16th century, there has been a castle in this location since the 13th. Continue past the youth hostel, field study centre and campsite to reach Arran Distillery, built in this location in 1995 on the recommendation of Glasgow University geologists to utilise the pure water of Loch na Davie nearby.

Take the path immediately after the distillery but before a small bridge to

follow the crystal clear burn through Gleann Easan Biorach. The path quickly becomes rough and bouldery and begins to rise past scenic waterfalls, eventually levelling out onto moorland. Progress is hampered by the need to avoid the worst patches of bog, and in places the faint path drops into fairly deep tributaries that may require a scramble out on the far side.

Further on, the gradient increases and the path becomes rocky underfoot as it aims for the bealach, soon reaching the shallow pool of Loch na Davie. Keep to the right of the loch and begin an ascent over the shoulder of Beinn Bhreac to reach a further bealach and the descent into Gleann Diomhan. Follow the obvious path on the east side of the burn for a pleasant descent to a deer fence – erected to protect rare species of trees from the attention of deer and sheep. The glen is home to the only two examples of Catacol whitebeam (*Sorbus pseudomeinichii*) in existence – making it the rarest tree in the UK. A third sapling was reputed to have been eaten by

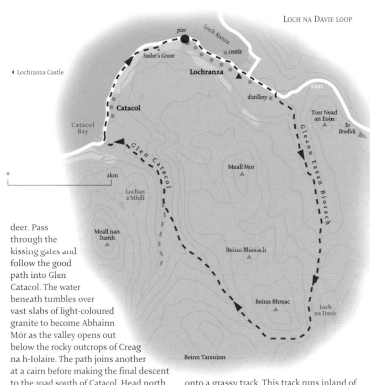

◄ Lochranza Castle

deer. Pass through the kissing gates and follow the good path into Glen Catacol. The water beneath tumbles over vast slabs of light-coloured granite to become Abhainn Mór as the valley opens out below the rocky outcrops of Creag na h-Iolaire. The path joins another at a cairn before making the final descent to the road south of Catacol. Head north along the quiet road and pass the cottages that form the Twelve Apostles – built to house crofters displaced by the Clearances. Each cottage was built with a different shaped upper window to allow fisherman offshore to identify candlelight signals from their families.

Passing the Catacol Bay Hotel, the road continues underneath the rugged cliffs dotted with caves and inhabited by nesting seabirds before branching right onto a grassy track. This track runs inland of the road at the foot of the cliffs to reach a mound of rocks with a simple inscribed rock headstone. The Sailor's Grave is the resting place of John McLean who was buried outwith the two neighbouring villages in 1854 for fear of introducing the plague into the populations. It is customary for travellers to add a pebble from the beach to the mound as a form of apology for his exclusion from the village graveyards. Follow the road back into Lochranza.

Loch Tanna from Catacol

Distance 14km **Time** 5 hours (return)
Terrain rough bouldery paths, very boggy
in places; a short section of quiet road
walking **Map** OS Explorer 361 or
Landranger 69 **Access** Stagecoach bus
(324) to Catacol

**A surprisingly rough and wild route to
remote Loch Tanna, Arran's biggest loch.**

Begin at the Catacol Bay Hotel at the
northern end of the small settlement of
Catacol. Follow the road south to reach a
roadbridge before a small car park and the
large white house named Fairhaven. Take

the footpath heading inland immediately
before the bridge, signposted 'Gleann
Diomhan and Loch Tanna'. This obvious
path shadows the river Abhainn Mór over
rocky outcrops and heather-coated knolls
before opening out into Glen Catacol.

Continue along the often boggy path as
the river begins to change character and
flow over vast granite slabs, forming
impressive rapids and waterfalls. Ignore
paths leading left into Gleann Diomhan
and onwards to Loch na Davie, keeping
right as you begin to climb towards the
head of the glen. Ford a series of small

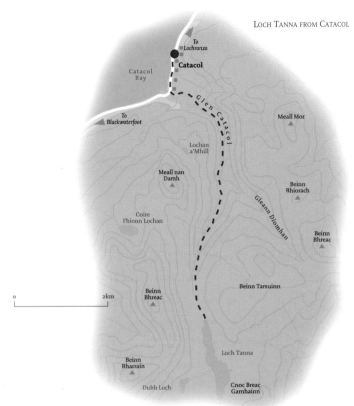

burns as the path becomes rockier and progress slows alongside the fast-flowing waters beneath Meall nan Damh.

The impressive waterfall of Allt nan Calman is a tempting place for a quick dip or just to stop and have a breather by. Carrying on from here, the path braids to avoid the worst of the saturated ground and the gradient increases, but your perseverance is rewarded when a large cairn and Loch Tanna, between the bulks of Beinns Tarsuinn and Bhreac, come into view. Continue over the watershed and, after a short descent, enjoy the golden sands of the loch shore.

Spend some time enjoying the solitude and silence of the largest and most remote loch on the island before returning by the same route.

◀ The Twelve Apostles, Catacol

Catacol and Lochan a'Mhill

Distance 4km **Time** 3 hours
Terrain faint and often boggy paths and
pathless moorland **Map** OS Explorer 361
or Landranger 69 **Access** Stagecoach bus
(324) to Catacol

A tough walk over rough – often pathless
– moorland. The initial ascent can be
severely hampered by bracken, so best to
attempt this walk once it has died down.
Your effort will be rewarded with
amazing views from this remote spot.

If approaching the car park from the
east you'll pass the Catacol Bay Hotel and
the Twelve Apostles, a row of almost
identical houses built in the 1860s to
re-house those displaced from Glen
Catacol in the Clearances. A short
distance after these, the road crosses a
bridge over crystal clear Abhainn Mór and
the car park is immediately after this on
the left.

Leave the car park by the obvious path
at the far end, which quickly becomes

grassy and overgrown as it dives through
the heather and bracken with the
Abhainn Mór tumbling below on its route
to Catacol Bay. Slowly ascending, the path
heads through a deer gate and then drops
to cross the Allt nan Eireannach via some
boulders before emerging at a meadow
watched over by a private camping barn.
Aim for this building, passing it on the
right, and take a narrow, wet path into
deciduous woodland.

The path is maintained by deer footfall
rather than human, and is pretty hard to
follow when the bracken is rampant.
If in doubt, remain parallel to the burn,
though safely back from the edge of the
deepening tree-lined gorge. As both the
ascent and tree cover begins to ease, watch
for a suitable place to cross the water.

On the far side, the path continues
straight ahead to meet a more obvious
way across the moorland. Turn left to
remain parallel to the burn on a path
which forks soon after the Allt nan

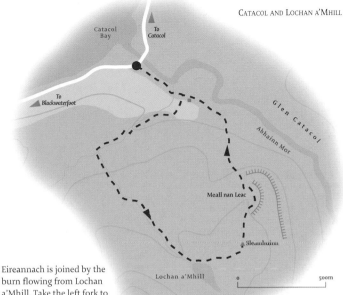

Catacol
Bay

To
Catacol

To
Blackwaterfoot

Glen Catacol

Abhainn Mor

Meall nan Leac

Sleamhuinn

Lochan a'Mhill

0   500m

Eireannach is joined by the burn flowing from Lochan a'Mhill. Take the left fork to cross by the stepping stones. On the far side, follow any semblance of a track uphill, now adjacent to this burn, looking for a suitable place to cross after 300m or so. The ascent continues beneath the rock face of Creagan nan Gobhar on the left, until a more obvious path appears for the final climb to the lochan. The rugged peaks of A'Chir and Caisteal Abhail emerge as you wind through the heather, before beautiful Lochan a'Mhill finally comes into view over the brow of the hill.

Descend to the lochside – an ideal place for lunch – and turn left for a short distance before crossing the heather-clad slopes of Meall nan Leac Sleamhuinn to the small summit cairn at 272m. This is a

fabulous viewpoint with Gleann Diomhan, home of the rarest tree in the UK, and Glen Catacol split by the steep slopes of Beinn Tarsuinn. Turn left to follow the ridge a short way north before bearing slightly right to avoid the granite slabs and carefully descend on animal tracks towards the valley floor.

Cross the burn whenever you can to reach a very wet path on the valley floor. This leads around, and through, a series of boggy pools before heading into bracken to reach the meadow crossed at the beginning of the route. Cross the field and back over the burn to return to the car park.

◀ Lochan a'Mhill

Coire Fhionn Lochan

Distance 5.5km **Time** 2 hours
Terrain grass and aggregate footpaths
with a few rocky sections
Map OS Explorer 361 or Landranger 69
Access Stagecoach bus (324) to
Thundergay

**A walk through moorland to a
beautiful mountain lochan with a white
gravel beach.**

There is limited parking opposite the
access road to the tiny settlement of
Thundergay. There are a few spaces
further north by the Allt Mòr bridge, and
these should be utilised in preference to
driving up the lane towards the houses.

A signpost indicates the route up the
track, which rises before curving left and
passing the last house by a gate, also
signposted. Go through the gate and onto
the gently sloping grassy path which
traverses the bracken-clad slope heading
roughly northeast towards one of the
tributaries of the Allt Mòr. Cross a ladder
stile adjacent to a deer fence, with the
wooded glen of the Allt Mòr visible ahead.

The path could now be a bit muddy,
before improving significantly thanks to
recent restorative work. Cross the burn via
large stepping stones and turn sharp

right, the Uisge Soluis Mhóir now briefly on your right before the good path leads to another small ford. Cross this easily and the path almost immediately becomes rockier, with a rock staircase winding through bracken and heather.

At the summit of the staircase, the route leads over a series of granite slabs – potentially slippery in wet conditions – as the burn tumbles over similar slabs on the left. The going soon eases again on the well-constructed path, and the slopes of Meall Biorach and Meall Bhig draw the eye towards the corrie. Carry on along the pale gravel path to be met with a beautiful vista as Coire Fhionn Lochan comes into view. Take a break on the white beach before retracing your steps or continuing on to the neighbouring peaks.

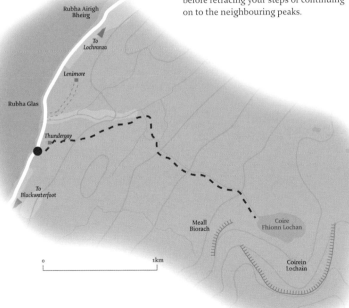

◀ Meall Biorach above Coire Fhionn Lochan

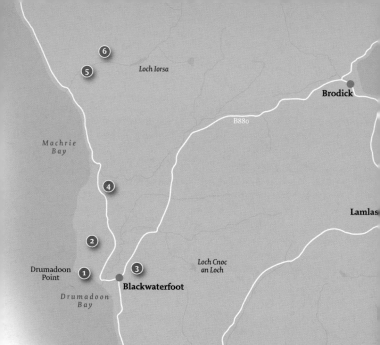

Blackwaterfoot is home to the celebrated 12-hole Shiskine golf course, and the noise of the ageing bus trundling over the String Road from Brodick is often supplemented by the sound of rattling golf clubs. A short walk along the pleasant sandy beach is Drumadoon Point, home to the largest iron age fort on Arran. Further north is the King's Cave, reputed to be a hiding place of Robert the Bruce, and atmospheric Machrie Moor – the site of a number of Bronze Age stone circles thought to be around 4500 years old.

As well as these straightforward walks,

this chapter features a rough ascent of Sail Chalmadale, where an easy estate track is left behind for a faint and often boggy path across moorland to reach the crag-ringed summit. The forest and moorland surrounding Shiskine is often neglected in favour of the honeypot peaks and ridges in the north, but this relative obscurity is rewarded by some wonderfully remote – if often boggy – walking. From here, the route to Loch Cnoc an Loch, though lacking in height gain, requires sound judgement and a higher level of navigation ability.

Blackwaterfoot and the west

Drumadoon Point and The Doon

Distance **4km** Time **2 hours**
Terrain **sandy beach, grassy footpaths
and golf course paths; a stretch of easy
boulder hopping beneath the Doon**
Map **OS Explorer 361 or Landranger 69**
Access **Stagecoach buses to
Blackwaterfoot**

A pleasant circuit along the shoreline
west of Blackwaterfoot, crossing a
boulderfield beneath the impressive
columnar basalt cliffs of the Doon. The
return leg offers extensive views from
the summit plateau.

There is a public car park adjacent to the
golf course west of Blackwaterfoot. Leave
this and either walk along the beach itself
or the parallel path running between the
golf course and beach. A junction at the
end of the path indicates a route to King's
Cave by turning right; ignore this and

turn left onto the beach (unless you are
already on it). Cross a burn and continue
along the sand towards the rocky
headland of Drumadoon Point, with
views across the Kilbrannan Sound to
Davaar Island guarding the entrance to
Campbeltown Loch.

Go round the point and continue right
along a grassy path over rocky outcrops to
reach a view indicator before heading over
larger outcrops and onto the tip of the
golf course. Cross to a gate in the far fence
– looking out for golfers and golf balls –
and pass through to the narrow, grassy
path beyond. This leads towards a large
boulderfield beneath the towering

To
King's Cave

The
Doon

standing
stone

0   500m

golf
course

Drumadoon

Drumadoon
Point

Blackwaterfoot

D r u m a d o o n
B a y

columnar basalt cliffs of the Doon. There is the option of scrambling up to a path directly below the cliffs, but it's fairly straightforward to trace a path through and over the boulderfield on the grippy rock. There are a couple of small cairns indicating the easiest route through the boulders, but a small grassy path is soon reached at the far end.

Follow this into the deep grass and bracken to meet the path heading south from King's Cave and turn right. This path climbs steeply around the northern end of the Doon, before crossing the field boundary via a gate. Go through this onto a track over farmland, keeping an eye out

for a grassy trod leading uphill towards the summit plateau. Follow this through the remains of a rock and earth rampart and then go through a gate to emerge in tall grasses, harebells and tormentil. Spend some time enjoying the summit views and the standing stones before retracing your steps to the gap in the ramparts and returning to the grass track. Turn right and follow the path to a stile with an Arran Coastal Way waymarker; cross this and descend to the golf course thoroughfare. Turn left to skirt along the northern boundary of the golf course, passing the tennis courts and clubhouse to reach the car park.

◀ Rock flora at Drumadoon Point

King's Cave coastal walk

Distance 6km **Time** 3 hours (one way)
Terrain beaten earth woodland tracks
and potentially rough beach walking,
followed by good golf course paths
Map OS Explorer 361 or Landranger 69
Access Stagecoach bus (324) to car park
3km north of Blackwaterfoot

A fine coastal walk taking in a series of
caves in sandstone cliffs, including the
historic King's Cave in which Robert the
Bruce is said to have had his legendary
encounter with a spider. This walk can be
completed in either direction, using the
bus from Blackwaterfoot, or form part of
a circuit which returns via the quiet A841.
A shorter 5km circuit returns to the car
park just after King's Cave.

Take the path from the far right corner
of the signposted car park and skirt the

northern boundary of the forest. You are
soon rewarded with views across the
Kilbrannan Sound to the Kintyre
Peninsula. The path curves left before
dropping down a switchback through a
cleft in the rock to a gate; go through this
onto the seashore. Now bearing south,
the path may occasionally disappear, so
look for the easiest – or most interesting
– route along the rocky foreshore.

The caves eventually appear in the cliffs
to the left; King's Cave is easily identified
by its large metal entrance gate, originally
intended to protect the Christian and pre-
Christian carvings inside. It appears to be
kept open most of the time, but it's
obviously still important to avoid damage
to the carvings. It also lays claim to being
the site where the exiled Robert the Bruce,
seeking refuge after his defeat by the
English in 1307, was inspired by a spider's

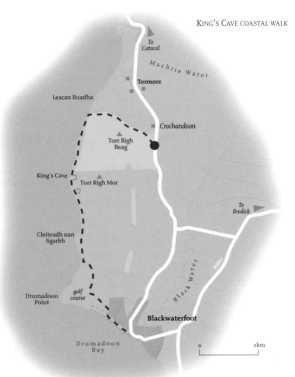

To
Catacol

Machrie Water

Tormore

Leacan Ruadha

Crochandoon

Torr Righ
Beag

King's Cave

Torr Righ Mor

To
Brodick

Cleiteadh nan
Sgarbh

Black Water

B880

Drumadoon
Point

golf
course

Blackwaterfoot

Drumadoon
Bay

0   1km

repeated efforts to spin a web against the odds. This restored Robert's motivation to continue with his campaign, concluding with the victory at Bannockburn in 1314.

Leaving the cave, turn left and explore the remainder of the caverns before returning to your route along the beach. Ignore the signposted path heading left through the bracken (unless you have left your car in the woodland car park, as this is where it leads). Instead, continue along

a grassy raised beach with the cliffs of the Doon ahead. Immediately before you come to the cliffs, the path starts to climb abruptly; follow it to reach a gate and a grassy path heading across a field. This leads you downhill to the stile on the golf course boundary fence. Turn left and proceed along the main path, skirting the edge of the golf course as directed, to reach the clubhouse and the metalled road into Blackwaterfoot.

◀ The Doon

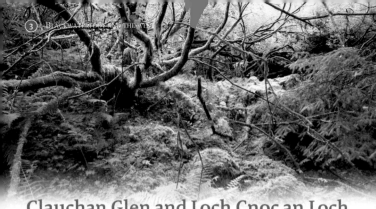

Clauchan Glen and Loch Cnoc an Loch

Distance 11km **Time** 3 hours
Terrain grassy footpaths and forest rides,
potentially muddy in places
Map OS Explorer 361 or Landranger 69
Access Stagecoach bus (322) to Shiskine

A rough circular walk through forest and moorland, starting from the village of Shiskine on Thomas Telford's String Road. The ford over the Clauchan Water can be impassable after heavy rain.

There is on-street parking in the village of Shiskine, but please be considerate. Head out of Shiskine along the String Road – surveyed and designed by legendary civil engineer Thomas Telford – northeast towards Brodick. Keep with the road as it bends sharply left to cross a bridge over the Clauchan Water, then passes a small campsite. Take the road on the right immediately after this, climbing uphill to reach a cemetery.

Soon after this, the surfaced road becomes a firm forestry track which passes a small cottage and continues to rise. Look out for a small path leading off to the right and follow this as it descends to meet the river at a rocky ford. After heavy rain, the river may be high and the ford non-existent, so exercise caution.

A narrow grass footpath leads into the trees from the river – accompany this as it zigzags up through the woodland, occasionally offering glimpses to the river below in Clauchan Glen, but generally tightly corralled within the tall forestry. As the forest thins at a heathery clearing, take a sharp right turn by a waymarker post and continue climbing. Eventually the ascent eases, but in several places fallen branches have completely blocked the path and detours into the forest become necessary. Cross a small burn and carry on along a forest ride to reach a gate in the forest with open moorland beyond. It is possible to cross this and follow the path onwards to Glenree on the Ross Road, but this route turns right to proceed between the forest and fence. Carpeted in sphagnum moss, this section

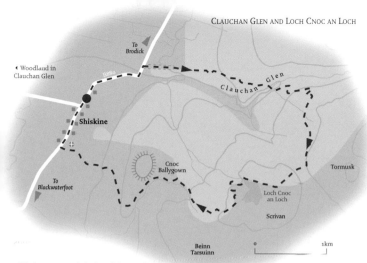

will almost certainly be a bit wet, but it is possible to weave a route which avoids the worst areas.

Serious hillbaggers can cross the fence and make the brief ascent to the summit of Scrivan; otherwise continue downhill to the superbly named Loch Cnoc an Loch. Continue over the moorland between the loch and the forest, and curve left to follow the western shore along the occasional traces of an ATV track. Just before curving around the southern bank of the loch, look out for tracks heading into the trees along a forest ride. This grassy track leads through the tall trees for a short distance before meeting a larger forest ride. Turn left and then right onto a more defined path that curves gently right to meet a burn and then downhill to reach a gate in the forest boundary. Pass through this onto a good track along the bottom of a valley

between the hill fort of Cnoc Ballygown and one of several Beinn Tarsuinns on Arran. The track crosses a small burn a few times before reaching a gate with a signpost signalling the ascent path to the unfinished hill fort of Cnoc Ballygown; there is not much to see on the summit, apart from a good view of the northern mountains and the Kintyre Peninsula.

Continue through the gate and follow the obvious path, soon flanked by gorse bushes but still offering good views over Blackwaterfoot and Kilbrannan Sound. Go through another gate in a line of beech trees and turn sharply left to descend right, then left and pass through a couple more gates to reach the farm at Balgowan. Take the farm access road and drop down past the mobile phone mast to the road. Turn right at the road past the 'Red Kirk' of St Molios to return to the start.

69

Machrie Moor Stone Circles

Distance 4km **Time** 2 hours (return)
Terrain a combination of good farm
tracks merging with grassy footpaths
Map OS Explorer 361 or Landranger 69
Access Stagecoach bus (324) to car park
5km north of Blackwaterfoot

**A there-and-back walk to explore
atmospheric standing stones in a bleak
moorland setting.**

Start from the signposted car park 5km
north of Blackwaterfoot on the A841.
Cross the road to pass through the hedge
as the signpost indicates and go over the
stile to proceed up the wide, grassy path
to a gate/stile. Beyond this, the path
continues to the melodic accompaniment
of the Machrie Water, one of Arran's two
salmon rivers, audible from the far side of
the woodland to the left.

The path makes a sharp right, then left,
and the first cairn is visible over a fence to
the right. There is a detailed information
board located close enough to the fence

to negate the need to clamber over the
remains. Continuing along the path, the
ruins of Moss Farm come into view, along
with the double stone ring of Suide Choir
Fhionn, or Fingal's Cauldron Seat, named
after the legendary warrior. Legend has it
that Fingal tied his dog Bran to the stone
with the hole in the outer ring whilst
cooking a meal in the inner circle.

Ignore the track leading towards the
ruinous buildings and instead cross to a
gate and two information boards off to
the right, with views to the most
impressive standing stones beyond. Go
through the gate and out onto the
moorland, particularly atmospheric when
shrouded in mist.

A network of small paths leads between
the various groups of stones which
include several free-standing red
sandstone slabs; the tallest is over 5m
high. The most intact of the circles
consists of three upright pillars with the
other stones that make up the circle

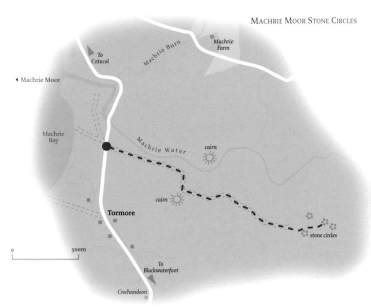

fallen. Notice that two of the granite boulders within the circle have been carved into millstones. Another tall pillar close to the abandoned farmstead appears to exist in isolation but is, in fact, part of a larger circle; the other stones have been removed or lie buried.

Although the stone circles date from the Bronze Age period (1800-1600BC), archaeological excavations suggest the site was in use in the Neolithic period. Several timber circles were erected on the moor in the general area of the current stone circles. The main circle consisted of about 50 tall wooden posts with an inner ring of taller posts in a horseshoe formation. After a long period of activity, the site seems to have returned to

agricultural usage before the construction of the stone circles began around 1800BC.

In common with many stone circles of this era, evidence suggests that this site has an astronomical function relating to the phases of the sun and moon; the changing seasons being of great importance to ancient man. A site survey in 1978 suggested that the stone circles were in general alignment with a notch on the skyline where Machrie Glen forks. This notch is intersected by the sun on Midsummer's morning – the longest day of the year and the beginning of the countdown to winter.

Enjoy exploring the site and absorbing the atmosphere before returning by the same route.

Glen Iorsa

Distance 7.5km **Time** 3 hours (return)
Terrain rough earth footpaths and well-made estate track; one shallow ford
Map OS Explorer 361 or Landranger 69
Access Stagecoach bus (324) to Dougarie

A pleasant, easy walk along a scenic glen to the boathouse at the foot of Loch Iorsa.

Dougarie Lodge have made it clear that Glen Iorsa is not to be accessed via the main entrance track and have provided a well-signposted footpath leading directly away from the lay-by adjacent to the A841. Follow the surfaced track uphill past farmland until it turns left, then ascend the eroded rocky steps straight ahead to reach a ladder stile. Cross this and turn left along an obvious grassy path. Cross another stile and pass through scrubland before entering a patch of pleasant deciduous woodland. Leaving the wood, the path runs through dense bracken waymarked with black and white posts – and with a selection of boggy patches.

The path eventually reaches the main estate track into the glen, with the old shooting lodge well bypassed. Almost immediately, the track leads over a shallow concrete ford; thankfully there is a good wooden footbridge too. Cross the Allt na h-Airighe and enjoy the well-made track beyond, which gives excellent views down the glen to Beinn Tarsuinn and Beinn Nuis. Further along the glen, pass through a deer gate to a ford over the

Scaftigill Burn – this time without the luxury of a footbridge after it was swept away during a storm. A constant companion for the early part of this walk, the Iorsa Water is one of Arran's two salmon rivers and divided into 16 pools over two beats by a series of weirs.

Just after crossing the shallow ford, you'll see a small path on the left marked by a tiny cairn. This leads over the rough moorland to the summit of Sail

Chalmadale via a couple of pleasant mountain lochs (see page 74). For this route, however, continue on the obvious track along the broad, empty glen for a further 1.5km to reach the boathouse at the foot of Loch Iorsa. A path continues further along the loch, but it is boggy and soon disappears. Far better to spend some time enjoying the scenery before retracing your steps to the start.

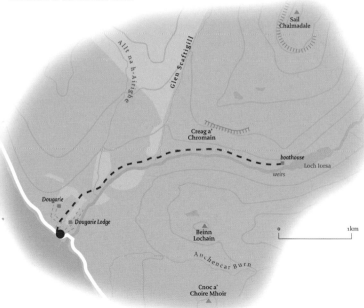

Sail Chalmadale

Distance 11km **Time** 5 hours 30
Terrain earth footpaths, well-made estate
tracks and rough moorland path; one
shallow ford **Map** OS Explorer 361 or
Landranger 69 **Access** Stagecoach bus
(324) to Dougarie

**A rough mountain walk to a granite-
studded peak via two remote lochs.**

Dougarie Lodge have made it clear that
Glen Iorsa is not to be accessed via the
main entrance track and have provided a
signposted footpath leading directly away
from the lay-by adjacent to the A841.
Follow the surfaced track uphill past
farmland until it turns left, then ascend
the eroded rocky steps straight ahead to
reach a ladder stile. Cross this and turn
left along an obvious grassy path. Cross
another stile and pass through scrubland
before entering a patch of pleasant
deciduous woodland. Leaving the wood,

the path runs through dense bracken
waymarked with black and white posts –
and with a selection of boggy patches.

The path eventually reaches the main
estate track into the glen, with the old
shooting lodge well bypassed. Almost
immediately the track leads over a
shallow concrete ford; thankfully there is
also a good wooden footbridge. Cross the
Allt na h-Airighe and enjoy the well-made
track beyond, which gives views down the
glen to Beinn Tarsuinn and Beinn Nuis.
Further along the glen, pass through a
deer gate to a ford over the Scaftigill Burn
– this time without the luxury of a
footbridge after it was swept away during
a storm. A constant companion for the
early part of this walk, the Iorsa Water is
one of Arran's two salmon rivers and
divided into 16 pools over two beats by a
series of weirs.

Just after crossing the shallow ford, look

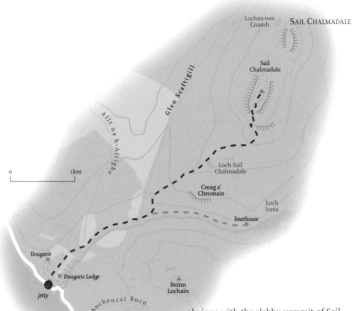

Lochan nan Cnamh

SAIL CHALMADALE

Glen Scaftigill

Sail Chalmadale

Allt na h-Airighe

Loch Sail Chalmadale

Creag a' Chromain

Loch Iorsa

boathouse

Dougarie

Dougarie Lodge

Beinn Lochain

jetty

Auchencar Burn

0   1km

out for a small path on the left marked by a tiny pale cairn. This takes you parallel to the burn for a short distance before meeting a faint ATV track and beginning the ascent up the tussocky hillside. Soon it splits, and a more obvious path contours to the left. Ignoring this, continue northeast up onto the main shoulder of Sail Chalmadale. Though the trail is often non-existent, it does reappear and the nature of the terrain makes forging a new path pretty difficult.

Perseverance is rewarded by the appearance of Loch Sail Chalmadale at 230m – around 3.5 km after leaving the path. From here, the trail should be quite

obvious with the slabby summit of Sail Chalmadale looming ahead. It is possible to deviate from the onward track to visit a smaller loch; otherwise continue to the foot of the granite slabs. Bear right, off the path, to avoid the vertical rock faces and begin a steep scramble up, over and through the bouldery slopes. The gradient eventually eases on the small heathery summit plateau, and an easy path leads through the boulders to the summit cairn at 480m. Enjoy the panoramic views over the island and to Kintyre, before retracing your steps into Glen Iorsa. Upon reaching the main track, it is worth expending any remaining energy by turning left to visit the boathouse at Loch Iorsa, 1.5km further on (see page 72).

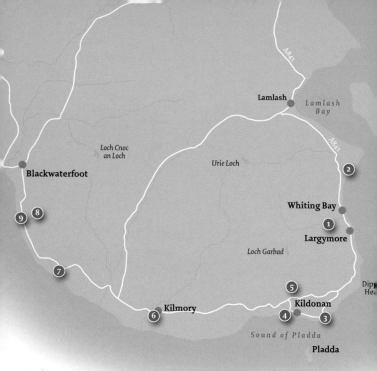

Southern Arran is characterised by rolling pastures and long sandy beaches. The largest village in this area is Whiting Bay – once the site of a substantial steamer pier which attracted an upmarket clientèle who built the grand villas lining the road. Modern Whiting Bay retains a quiet elegance, with many of the villas converted to guest accommodation.

At the southern end of the bay, the spectacular Glenashdale Falls tumble through woodland and combine with a nearby iron age fort and chambered cairns

known as the Giants' Graves to make one gentle walk.

Further south, Kildonan is celebrated for having what is probably the best beach on the island – a long stretch of sand with awesome views south, including to the small island of Pladda.

To the southwest, Kilmory – actually incorporating the settlements of Torrylinn and Lagg – houses a creamery where the famous Isle of Arran Cheese is produced. The numerous prehistoric settlements here are also evidence of far earlier habitation.

Whiting Bay and Southern Arran

Glenashdale Falls

Distance 4.5km **Time** 2 hours
Terrain metalled roads and rough tracks
Map OS Explorer 361 or Landranger 69
Access Stagecoach bus (323) to
Whiting Bay

**A circuit through a wooded glen to a
dramatic waterfall and iron age fort with
the option to detour and visit the
gravesite of ancient giants.**

Start from the southern end of Whiting
Bay alongside the Coffee Pot tearoom.
There is space to park alongside the
tearoom, though the excellent bus service
will also stop here. Walk uphill past the
restaurant on the metalled road as it
winds through the houses. Head straight
across at a signposted junction and

continue along the road as it becomes an
unsurfaced vehicle track.

Pass through a series of gates to enter
the woodland and cross a burn via a series
of large regular stepping stones. Follow
the path as it heads uphill into the forest
before taking a turning on the left
signposted 'Glenashdale Falls via Iron Age
Fort'. The path through the trees isn't
particularly easy to follow, but it
eventually arrives at a viewpoint
overlooking the glen and distant falls.
Turn around and take the path forking left
to cross a footbridge and arrive at the iron
age fort sitting in a prime defensive
location atop a rocky outcrop.

Continue along the path after exploring
the ruins and follow the green and white

◀ Glenashdale Falls

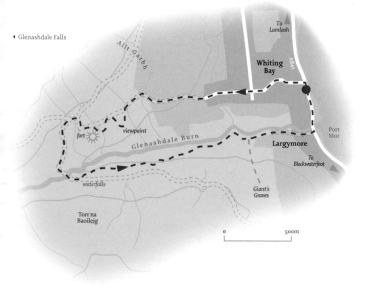

marker posts to reach the north side of the falls. Cross the footbridge immediately above the falls and turn left down the other side of the valley to reach a wooden viewing platform jutting out over the glen, offering a spectacular view of the double falls. This walk is best undertaken after a few days of heavy rain, when a huge volume of water will be gushing over the 45m waterfall via an intermediate plunge pool and into the river below.

Carry on along the track, ignoring any branches off the main route – though after around 1.5km, there is the option of visiting the Giants' Graves at a signposted

junction. This is a steep climb up 300 wooden steps to a high clearing containing an unusual array of upright stones guarding the remains of a Neolithic burial chamber; in local legend once containing the bones of ancient giants.

The main path continues alongside the burn to reach a wider track which eventually reaches the main road at the shore. Turn left to walk along the shore road above the wide sand and pebble beach at the southern end of Whiting Bay and onward to the Coffee Pot tearoom or further north and into town.

Kingscross Point from Whiting Bay

Distance 3km **Time** 1 hour 30
Terrain metalled roads, rough tracks and
shingle beach **Map** OS Explorer 361 or
Landranger 69 **Access** Stagecoach bus
(323) to Whiting Bay

**A short walk to the ruins of a Viking
fort with views to Holy Island and
Lamlash Bay.**

There is space to park alongside the
playing field at the northern end of
Whiting Bay, although the bus service will
also stop here. Walk past the church to
reach a fork in the road; take the left fork
to a small car park alongside the beach
before reaching a bridge over a burn.
Cross the bridge and turn immediately
right onto an unsurfaced road. Pass
several houses and head onto the beach
at the end of the track.

Walk along the beach, but keep an eye
out for a signposted path leaving it on the
left. Cross the stile and follow the narrow
path – occasionally boggy in places –
through high gorse bushes. Cross another
stile after a couple of stepping stones
through a particularly moist patch, and
enter a brief section of scrubby woodland.
Keep to the edge of the subsequent
grazing land before crossing a further stile
and returning to woodland.

Emerging from the trees, turn right
at a path junction cut through bracken to
reach a more open grassy area. Continue
straight ahead to eventually reach the low
ruins of the fort with views across to the
Buddhist retreat on Holy Island and
Lamlash Bay.

Excavations have shown that Kingscross
Point had been home to a dun or fortified

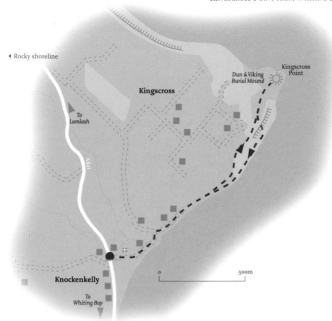

◀ Rocky shoreline

Kingscross

To
Lamlash

Dun & Viking
Burial Mound

Kingscross
Point

To
Whiting Bay

Knockenkelly

0   500m

homestead for around two thousand years before being used by the Vikings as a settlement and burial site. It has been suggested that the bay south of Kingscross Point was originally called 'Viking Bay' before being corrupted to Whiting Bay.

Kingscross Point has a further claim to fame, and one from which it takes its name; Robert the Bruce is said to have sailed to the mainland from here in February 1307, prior to defeating the English in battle at Loudoun that summer.

Return along the outward path to reach the open grassy area and take a small rough path heading downhill to the left. This descends to a shingle beach – turn right and follow this back to the start. On the way, watch out for the varied birdlife that inhabits this stretch of coast – curlew, oystercatcher and ringed plover and a range of gulls, including large numbers of kittiwakes in the early autumn. Ringed plover and oystercatchers are renowned for laying well-camouflaged eggs in small scrapes in the shingle – take care when walking above the high-tideline in late April and May.

Kildonan Castle

Distance 1km **Time** 30 mins
Terrain metalled roads, rough tracks and
sandy beach **Map** OS Explorer 361 or
Landranger 69 **Access** Stagecoach bus
(323) to east of Kildonan

**A short circular walk along a beautiful
sandy beach which then climbs to view
the ruins of Kildonan Castle.**

The walk begins from a small lay-by
suitable for a few cars (opposite a larger
grass car park). Proceed down a flight of
stairs towards an inviting sandy beach
overlooking the rocky island of Pladda
with its prominent white lighthouse built
by engineer Thomas Smith. Twice-
widowed Smith married the mother of

Robert Stevenson in 1787; young Robert
became his apprentice and founded the
famous lighthouse-building dynasty
whose work can be seen all around
Scotland's coastline. After completion of
the lighthouse in 1790, lightkeepers relied
on a small boat that visited the island
four times a month (but twice on a
Sunday to allow the keepers to attend
church). A helicopter replaced the boat in
1972, but the arrangement ended in 1990
when the lighthouse became automated
and monitored remotely from the
Northern Lighthouse Board headquarters
in Edinburgh.

The granite stump of Ailsa Craig is often
visible on the horizon beyond, home to a

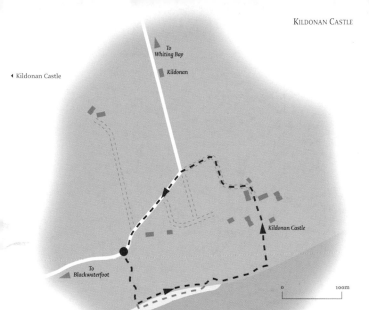

huge colony of gannets and the source of countless curling stones crafted from the blue hone granite.

Pass a small playground to reach the beach itself and turn left along an obvious path, or alternatively enjoy the feeling of sand between your toes by walking on the beach itself. Turning your back on Pladda, the ruins of Kildonan Castle come into view on the cliffs above – ideally situated with an unrestricted view across the Firth of Clyde it was erected to protect.

Built in the 13th century by the MacDonald clan, the castle's role soon changed to that of a hunting lodge for the Kings of Scotland, including Robert III. An obvious path leads up from the shore towards the cluster of private houses surrounding the ruins; follow this past an interpretive board for a closer look, but please respect the privacy of the householders.

Thread through the houses, trending left to reach the access drive and follow this back to the junction with the main road. Turn left and take the road back to the roadside lay-by and the start of the walk.

Kildonan shore

**Distance 4.3km Time 2 hours
Terrain metalled roads, rough tracks and
sandy beach Map OS Explorer 361 or
Landranger 69 Access Stagecoach bus
(323) to just past Kildonan**

**A linear walk along a rugged shoreline
below impressive cliffs with the
opportunity to see a variety of marine
wildlife at close quarters.**

Located at the southern tip of Arran,
Kildonan is named after the Irish monk
St Donan who is believed to have lived in
the area in the 6th century. St Donan is
also the patron saint of the Isle of Eigg;
he was martyred there by a Pictish queen
– along with 150 of his followers. Their
bodies were burnt, but his remains are
reputedly buried in the village.

The walk begins from a car park
adjacent to a prominent rocky outcrop.
Head west along the road, passing a war
memorial embedded in the rock, to reach
a minor road branching left as the main
road turns sharply inland. Take this track
as it heads towards the village's former
post office and shop, and continue
through a gate and onto a narrower
footpath. Watch out for the first of a series
of dramatic waterfalls tumbling over the
escarpment on the right.

Unusual igneous dykes are very much
in evidence at this point; projecting from
the sandy beach into the surf, you will
often see common seals lazing around on

top of them. To avoid disturbing the seals, please do not climb along these dykes. Pass an interpretive board outlining the varied wildlife found in the area and follow the path across the grassy raised beach corralled by steep cliffs to the right and the rocky beach to the left.

The rockpools in the intertidal area of the beach are a unique habitat for crabs, anemones and various seaweeds, and there is always the possibility of a basking shark cruising close to shore in pursuit of summer plankton blooms.

Turn around before reaching the boulderfield forming Struey Rocks; the going becomes quite difficult here in contrast to the easy terrain of the rest of the walk. Returning east affords panoramic views to the island of Pladda with its whitewashed lighthouse, and the hulk of Ailsa Craig beyond. Alisa Craig's huge colony of gannets can often be seen along the Arran coastline plunging into the sea from a great height in search of fish. Retrace your steps to the car park.

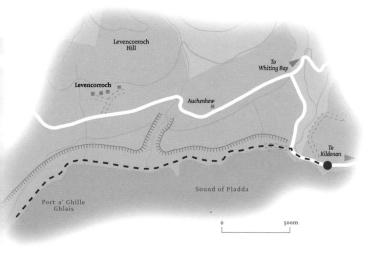

Eas Mor and Loch Garbad

Distance 5.5km **Time** 1 hour 30 to 2 hours
Terrain well-made all-abilities aggregate
footpaths as far as the waterfall, then a
rougher and slightly boggier path to the
loch **Map** OS Explorer 361 or Landranger
69 **Access** Stagecoach bus (323) to just
past Kildonan

A walk through forestry to view a
'Hidden Valley' and the dramatic Eas Mor
waterfall before reaching a remote and
peaceful hill loch.

There is a dedicated car park alongside
the A841 opposite the road down to
Kildonan. The bus will stop at this
junction if requested. Leave the car park
by the Eas Mor Ecology interpretive board
and donation box and enjoy the well-
made all-abilities track constructed by the
organisation. The gently rising path is
lined by a variety of native plants and
trees, with wildflowers punctuating the
verges below. It soon enters forestry
above a steep-sided gorge, deep enough
to prevent the Allt Mor at the valley base
from being viewed from here.

There are a number of viewing
platforms located along the path, but the
final platform offers the most dramatic
view of the long plume of the Eas Mor
waterfall plunging down the cliff face and
into the ravine far below. Leaving this
viewing station, a path forks left,
signposted 'Loch Garbad 1 mile'. Continue
along this rougher path skirting the forest

Loch Garbad

Cnoc na
Comhairle

Cnoc Craobhach

Cnoc na
Garbad

Torran
Clachach

Auchenhew
Hill

Ballymeanochglen

Eas Mor

To
Whiting Bay

Levencorroch
Hill

Levencorroch

Auchenhew

To
Blackwaterfoot

Kildonan

Porta
Buidhe

0   1km

boundary, with the tall conifers on the left and farmland to the right. Soon the path reaches a gate and stile on the right leading down to Ballymeanochglen and the farm beyond – ignore this and continue left to re-enter the forest.

The path follows a small watercourse as it continues gently uphill. Step over a small burn and enter a wider forest ride lined with heather, before reaching Loch Garbad by a small picnic bench. Popular with fly fishermen, this tranquil loch is a lovely place for a lunch break. Return to the junction above the waterfall, but make sure you stop into the Eas Mor Ecology library – a turf-roofed wooden structure built from trees felled in the 1998 storm and lined with drawings created by visitors. Return to the car park via the main track.

Kilmory beach circular

Distance 2.4km **Time** 1 hour
Terrain metalled roads, rough tracks and
sandy beach **Map** OS Explorer 361 or
Landranger 69 **Access** Stagecoach bus
(323) to Kilmory

**A short circular walk which takes in what
is probably Arran's best beach.**

The walk begins from a car park in
Kilmory adjacent to the village hall – with
attached bunkhouse and part-time post
office. Follow a signpost reading 'Torrylinn
Cairn' to head alongside the hall and into
the pleasant, lightly-wooded glen of the
Torrylinn Water. The well-made path leads
downhill to merge with another path from
the right; continue downstream on a
grassy, often boggy trail as it curves left to
skirt a drystane dyke and reach a small
burial cairn with accompanying
interpretive board.

Torrylinn Cairn is a Clyde cairn, a type of
ancient monument built in 3300BC to a
common pattern. This style of cairn has
been found in various locations across
southern Scotland – particularly, as the
name suggests, around the Clyde Valley
and Estuary. When originally built, this
type of cairn would have comprised a
large rectangular mound surrounded by a
layer of stones. One of the narrow ends of
the cairn would have been cut away to
form a concave face and lined with stone
to leave a paved area in front of the cairn.
A pair of upright stones would have
marked the entrance to a rectangular
burial chamber where the bones of the
corpse were deposited after being
defleshed; it is assumed that the forecourt
area was designed to hold a burial
ceremony. Torrylin Cairn has been badly
damaged by later farming, leaving a

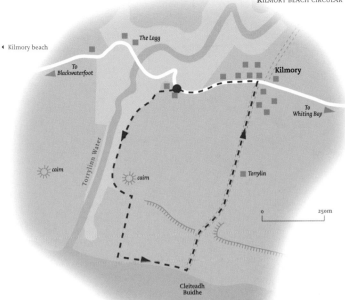

◀ Kilmory beach

The Lagg

To
Blackwaterfoot

Kilmory

To
Whiting Bay

Torrylinn Water

☀ caim

☀ caim

Torrylinn

0   250m

Cleiteadh
Buidhe

roughly circular mound with some of the stones that would have lined the burial chamber. An excavation in 1900 unearthed the remains of six adults and two children.

Beyond this, the path reaches a kissing gate on the right; go through and walk down through the field towards the shore. Cross a stile to reach the beautiful and quite often deserted beach. The granite stump of Ailsa Craig is visible on the horizon, as well as the Ayrshire coastline beyond. Stroll left as far as a concrete wall built into a rocky outcrop, and turn left up an obvious track.

This eventually takes you to the main road alongside the Torrylinn Creamery – home of the Highlands and Islands Cheese Company and award-winning cheese since it was built by the Milk Marketing Board in the 1940s. The distinctive Arran Dunlop cheese – creamier and less acidic than cheddar – is still made using traditional methods. Friesian cows from three local dairy farms supply milk to the creamery and the shop here is always worth a visit.

Turn left and follow the road back to the car park, or catch the bus from the bus stop immediately opposite.

Corriecravie and Torr a'Chaisteil

Distance 3.8km **Time** 1 hour 30
Terrain footpaths and farm tracks with
the return leg along a surfaced road
Map OS Explorer 361 or Landranger 69
Access Stagecoach bus (323) to
Corriecravie

**A shoreline circuit featuring an iron age
fortified homestead with panoramic
sea views.**

The parking area lies adjacent to a set of
children's swings at the western end of
Corriecravie. From here, head seaward
over a grassy rise to a memorial plaque
erected to commemorate a pilot and
gunner who lost their lives when their
aeroplane came down off the rocky coast.

Descend slightly right via a faint grassy
path to reach a broad farm track aiming
towards the shore. Cross a stile on the
right to access another track bearing WNW
between grazing land before dropping

down through a kissing gate and into
another field.

It can get boggy here so make your way
whatever way you can towards the shore
to pick up a faint path running right to
left above the beach. This will probably be
wet and churned up by cows, but it
becomes easier after a short distance.
Thread through a boulderfield to reach a
gate in a fence – pass this to the right and
follow the path as it runs adjacent to a
large reed bed. Follow the derelict wall
and fence on the left to reach a small bay
with a burn draining into the sea. Cross
the burn and go through a gate in the
fence on the left.

Torr a'Chaisteil is obvious straight
ahead, so set off across the field aiming
for the bottom left corner of the mound.
Go through a gate and turn right to follow
an easy track that curves up the southern
face of the hill to emerge just below the

summit at an information board.

It may be difficult to appreciate today just how impressive this fortified farmstead, also known as Corriecravie Dun, would have looked when occupied. It would have been full of people and livestock, enclosed by massive 12ft-high walls and a dry moat, with a bridge across to the entrance defended by a curved rampart at least 10ft thick. The passage of time, with much of the stone taken for construction elsewhere, has left only traces of its past use, but from the top

you can see why this site was chosen. Enjoy magnificent views to the Mull of Kintyre, Sanda Island and Ailsa Craig as you imagine the lives of those who stood here long before you.

Turn away from the dun and head across the fields, occasionally picking up a narrow path that seems to lead directly through the wettest patches. Finally, pass through a kissing gate and cross a driveway to reach the main road. Turn left and follow the road back to the start.

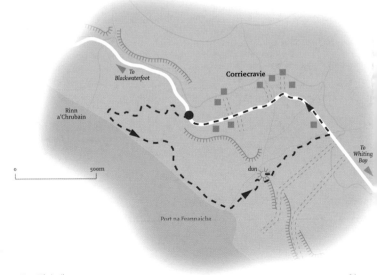

Kilpatrick Cashel

Distance 1.5km **Time** 1 hour
Terrain a good, if occasionally boggy,
grass track **Map** OS Explorer 361 or
Landranger 69 **Access** Stagecoach bus
(323) to Kilpatrick

**A short walk to the ruins of a circular
drystone homestead.**

Start out from the small walled car park
2km south of Blackwaterfoot. Turn left
out of the car park along the access road
for Kilpatrick Farm and take a small path
heading right at a black and white painted
post. Follow the track to a gate and stile;
cross over and follow the grassy path
across grazing land as directed by further
striped poles often supplemented with
arrows. Reach a further gate close to the

Allt a'Ghoirtean, pass through it and
follow the left fork beyond to climb more
steeply uphill onto the heather moorland.

As before, the route is indicated by a
plethora of striped poles snaking across
the moor – follow these to reach an oasis
of grass in the heather with the various
standing stones, turf walls and ridge and
furrow marks clearly visible. An
information board (facing the wrong way)
explains that the site is believed to be at
least 4000 years old and has been
modified and added to right into the
Middle Ages.

The name 'cashel' is an Anglicised form
of the Irish language word *caiseal*,
meaning 'stone ringfort'. Applied to this
site the term is misleading, as this isn't

actually a cashel. The archaeologist that excavated the site in the 1900s identified the confusing, muddled remains as similar to cashels found in Ireland used by early monastic communities. More recent studies suggest that this is, in fact, a dun, or fortified farmstead, built around 1800 years ago but significantly altered since. As the name 'Kilpatrick Cashel' has occurred on maps and signs for more than a hundred years it seems to have stuck.

The site offers extensive views across to the large fort of The Doon above Blackwaterfoot, as well as the Mull of Kintyre and Ireland beyond. Once the full hectare of land has been explored, ignore the poles and follow a path heading directly towards Blackwaterfoot to pick up a larger path running left to right and return to the path junction at the gate. Retrace your steps from this point to the car park.

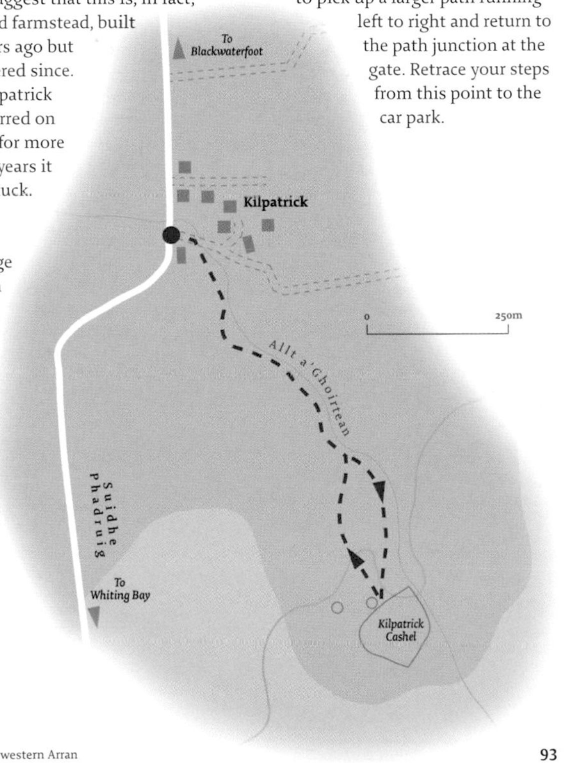

To
Blackwaterfoot

Kilpatrick

Allt a' Ghoirtean

0   250m

Suidhe
phadruig

To
Whiting Bay

Kilpatrick
Cashel

Kilpatrick Preaching Cave

Distance 2km **Time** 1 hour
Terrain a good, if occasionally boggy,
footpath **Map** OS Explorer 361 or
Landranger 69 **Access** Stagecoach bus
(323) to Kilpatrick

**A short coastal walk to a large cave once
used for religious services.**

Cross the main road from the car park
2km south of Blackwaterfoot and pass
through a gate alongside the Allt
a'Ghoirtean. Follow the gorse-lined track
across a ford via the stepping stones to
reach a field on the raised beach with the
rocky shore beyond. Go through a gate
onto a narrow grassy strip above the
beach and turn left.

The path leads towards the low cliffs
that grow in grandeur as the walk

continues and are studded with small
caves beyond the dense bracken and
goldenrod. The Preaching Cave is the
largest cave and indicated by a well-
trodden path and helpful arrow on a
wayside boulder. The full extent of the
cave can only be appreciated by close
investigation; the soot-blackened roof
indicates sustained use through the ages.

Following the unrest caused by the
19th-century Highland Clearances, where
entire villages were evicted by the Earl of
Arran to make way for large-scale sheep
grazing, the local people showed their
disaffection in the only way they could; by
rejecting the Earl's choice of minister for
their church congregation. The Preaching
Cave provided a meeting place for the
community as 'the Disruption of 1843'

◂ The Preaching Cave

took hold across the country. This schism in the established Church of Scotland was sparked by a sermon at St Giles Cathedral in Edinburgh from Dr Welsh, departing Moderator of the General Assembly. During the bitter conflict, 450 ministers left the established Church in protest at the actions of landowners and their disregard for their people; on Arran, churches emptied and the popular Free Church chose their own minister by appointing William McKinnon – a crofter who had himself been made homeless by the Clearances – as their preacher and pastor.

Leave the cave and continue along the shore path as desired – but bear in mind that the path becomes particularly rough after the headland of Rubha Garbhard. Return via the outward route with superb views along the coast to Kilpatrick Point and Drumadoon Bay beyond.

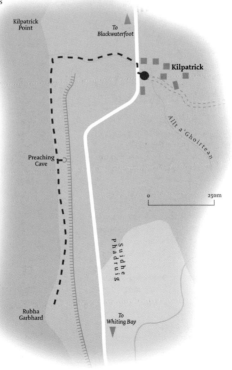

Index